MYSTIC SEAPORT
MOVEABLE FEASTS
COOKBOOK

EDITED BY GINGER SMYLE

ILLUSTRATED BY SALLY FISHER

COMMENTS BY ROSALIE MAXHAM

PUBLISHED BY MYSTIC SEAPORT MUSEUM STORES
MYSTIC, CT

Net income earned from *Mystic Seaport's Moveable Feasts Cookbook* will go toward supporting the programs at Mystic Seaport Museum, a non-profit educational institution.

For additional copies of *Mystic Seaport's Moveable Feasts Cookbook*, use the Order Blank in the back of the book or write directly to: Mystic Seaport Museum Stores
Bookstore
Mystic, CT 06355

or for credit card orders:
Call Toll Free (800) 331-BOOK (2665)
in Conn. (203) 572-8551

Suggested retail price: $14.95 + $4.00 for packing and shipping charges. (Connecticut residents add State Sales Tax.)

The *Moveable Feasts Cookbook* may be obtained by organizations for fund-raising projects or by retail outlets at special rates. Write to the above address for all of the details or call the above number.

Designed and typeset by Mim-G Studios, Inc.

ISBN 0-939510-14-6

First printing 1992
Second printing 1993

CONTENTS

INTRODUCTION

Ernest Hemingway described Paris as a Moveable Feast. He concluded that having lived there as a young man, it left a profound, indelible impression upon him and stayed with him wherever he went.

Mystic, Connecticut, is a similarly enchanting place. It provides those of us who live here with a satisfying nourishment of soul. Its picturesque scenery, memorable traditions and seagoing heritage comprise a moveable feast which serves as a meaningful backdrop for the rest of our lives.

It seemed only appropriate, then, that we entitle this cookbook *Moveable Feasts*. Not only did that title capture the depth of our feelings for this exquisite seacoast community, but, it also aptly described the types of recipes included here and the theme of this particular book.

Visiting Mystic Seaport is just one of the marvelous adventures in this area. Our cup of expeditions overfloweth, and we wanted a cookbook with recipes to reflect this — recipes that could accompany you on all the outings and innings of your life. We selected recipes easy to prepare and easily transported, but so wonderful that they, in themselves, would be a memorable enhancement to your adventures.

Moveable Feasts is organized into 20 themes. Thus, in addition to recipe suggestions, there are also ideas for fun occasions you may not have considered. Each section gives you a sample menu of recipes, and then the recipes are listed in familiar categories. You may pick and choose from these. Some recipe titles in the sample menus have been changed to relate to the themes while others have remained as contributed.

We have continued the tradition of excellence established by the previous Seaport cookbooks, testing and tasting hundreds of recipes reflecting the delectable food and wonderful lifestyle found in New England. Of course, even before recipes were tested, we knew it had passed a taste test in the home of the contributor.

The best foods were selected to take along and edited recipes make them easy to follow. You will notice that, for your convenience, the ingredients are listed in order to coincide with the numbered steps of preparation. In short, the work was done so you could have the fun. For fun is, after all, the message we want you to receive from this cookbook. Food *is* fun! It enriches any occasion. Preparation, presentation and eating should always be enjoyable experiences. The only limits are your imagination. So, pick up your *Moveable Feasts*, share it with others and, most importantly, have fun with it!

Happy Feasting!

Ginger Smyle

RECIPE CONTRIBUTORS

A special thank you to all the Friends and Members of Mystic Seaport who made this cookbook possible.

John and Binti Ackley
Ann Ahamed
Chandra Ahamed
Grace Anderson
Mary Lou Andrias
Lee Baker
Norman and Gail Bayne
Barbara Bergman
Mina Betancourt
Heather Bobbitt
Bolles Family
Kristan and Robert Bourestom
Mrs. Lloyd Boyden
Holly J. Bradshaw
Harriet Brown
Jim Brown
Randy Brown
Ann Burdick
Janet Caddle
Judith C. Camp
Lee Ann Chapman
Susan Chernesky
Marian Chichester
Sue Chojnacki
Joan Christensen
Mrs. Frederic S. Claghorn
Julie Coduri
Shirley Coleman

Vicki A. Collins
Jerilynn C. Comstock
Mrs. John Coward
Mary Crippen
Barbara K. Curphey
Winona Davis
Dr. and Mrs. Michael Deren
Susan Dinoto
Ann Douglas
Joseph Dubin
Doris A. Duggan
Susan Dunn
David Eaton
Teej Eaton
Joanie Elbourn
Lynne Ensign-Kaeser
Annice Estes
Susan Evans
Janice Fitton
Ceil Forman
Dana Forwood
Mary Galuska
Roger Galuska
Gloria C. Gavert
Arnold C. Gay
Judy Georg
Carol Geluso
June Getchius

Capt. L. W. Goddu, Jr.
Seija Goldstein
Barbara Goodwin
Julia Gottberg
Gail Marshall Grandgent
Rae Anna Gray
Tiffany Gray
Barbara J. Grebenstein
Senator George Gunther, N.D.
Sandy Halsey
Kathleen Hanning
Amy A. Harnish
Amy Havens
Sandra E. Herdendorf
Capt. and Mrs. Michael Hewitt
Michael Hoben
Nancy Holstein
Greta Jacobs
Cathy Jensen
Lance Johnson
Patty Johnson
Lee Ann Johnston
Lori Johnston
Marge Johnston
Carol Keemon
Andrea Kelmachter
Dalmar Kittredge
Dudley Knappe

Toni Kohl
Marilyn Kollmeyer
Mrs. Mona Kolocotronis
Julia La Pietra
Caroline Larson
Mary Lou Lemaire
Margaret Lewis
Catherine Litwin
Robert Logelin
Dorrie Long
Penny Magin
Judy Maher
Donna Marr
Martha L. Mason
Carmen Matlega
Lenore Mattoff
Rosalie Maxham
Sherri and Alister McGibbon
George Middleton
Stephen and Toni Miley
Bonita Mockler
David and Nancy Morton
Patricia O'Brien
Susan O'Donnell
Beth Olmstead
Mrs. Donald W. Olson
Mrs. Richard Palmer
Irene M. Patterson

Joyce Payer
Meredith Pedler
Jean Petryshyn
Jane Piché
Sue Pinzuti
Jo Plant
Pat Pocius
Phyllis Pray
Richard E. Raso
Laurie and David Rayner
Lena Reale
Barbara Repko
Nancy R. Richartz
Rosemarie Riechel
Mrs. Robert Ritzie
Angie Robinson
Peter Rosenberg, MD
Terri Rousseau
Alice Rowley
Patricia Savage
Mrs. Roger Scaife
Clara E. Schweiger
Victor Scottron
Helen Shaffer
Alan and Patricia Shapiro
Michael H. Sherwood
Donna Simpson
Jean Simpson

Caroline M. Sipp
Linda and Rick Skehan
Mrs. Allen Smith
Kathleen S. Smith
Dana Smyle
Michael Smyle
Stacy Smyle
Alice Solovy
Janie Stanley
Brooke Steinle
Bette Stickney
Amelia and Katherine Tanella
Nancy Tapley
Charles Teetor
Mary Thayer
Elizabeth Thève
Joan MacGregor Thorp
Frank Tito
Joseph Vrooman
Eleanor Walker
Isabel Wilson
Stephanie Wilson
Judy Woodman
Myrna Gale Wyse
Jacqueline Butler Zeppieri
Pat Ziegler

A very special thanks to Dede Wirth and Marge Johnston for production assistance.

BREAKFAST IN BED

SAMPLE MENU

Lullabies

Wake Up Waffles

Cozy Quilt Compote

Blueberry Puffs with Lemon Blanket

Herb Tea
or
Flavored Coffee

Why wait for Mother's Day, Father's Day, or a special holiday to enjoy breakfast in bed? This is a luxury to indulge in often. Our tested recipes ensure that even the most hard-boiled morning-haters will arise on the right side of the bed and be sunny-side-up all day. . . . So, prop up those pillows and resolve to treat yourself to our sumptuous selections. Don't waffle on your decision, just greet the bright new sunrise with a smile.

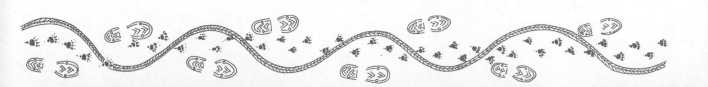

Banana Pancakes

Makes 12 pancakes

Don't just think banana bread — think Banana Pancakes!

2 cups flour
¼ cup sugar
½ teaspoon salt
1 tablespoon baking powder
3 tablespoons oil
1 cup orange juice
1 egg, beaten
2 bananas, sliced

1. In a medium bowl, mix flour, sugar, salt and baking powder.
2. Add oil, orange juice and beaten egg; mix well.
3. Fold in banana slices.
4. Heat lightly greased griddle to medium high.
5. Pour batter onto griddle using approximately ¼ cup batter for each pancake. Cook until bubbles appear. Flip pancakes over and cook until done.

Serve hot with butter and syrup.

Blueberry Cornmeal Pancakes

Serves 6 to 8

A remedy for those who get up on the wrong side of the bed.

1 cup flour
1 cup cornmeal
½ teaspoon salt
2 tablespoons baking powder
3 tablespoons sugar
3 tablespoons vegetable oil
1 egg, beaten
1½ cups orange juice
1 cup fresh or frozen blueberries, thawed

1. In a medium bowl, mix together flour, cornmeal, salt, baking powder and sugar.
2. Add oil, egg, juice; mix well.
3. Fold in blueberries.
4. Heat lightly greased medium-size griddle to medium high.
5. Pour batter onto griddle using approximately ¼ cup batter for each pancake. Cook until bubbles appear. Flip pancakes over and cook until done.

Serve with hot blueberry syrup.

Cottage Cheese Pancakes

Serves 2 to 4

Dare to be different.

1 cup cottage cheese
½ cup flour
4 eggs
6 tablespoons butter, melted

1. Preheat griddle.
2. Combine cottage cheese, flour and eggs in food processor.
3. Process briefly to mix.
4. Add butter; process until blended. Batter should be slightly lumpy.
5. Drop by quarter-cups onto the griddle.
6. Cook for 1½ to 2 minutes until bubbles appear.
7. Flip and cook other side.

Serve with a flavored yogurt.

Oatmeal Buttermilk Pancakes

Serves 4 to 6

Sleep later in the morning with a little preparation the night before.

½ cup water
½ cup instant powdered milk
1 tablespoon honey
1½ cups rolled oats
2 cups buttermilk
2 eggs, beaten
1 cup whole wheat flour
1 teaspoon baking soda
½ teaspoon salt

1. The night before serving: mix water, powdered milk and honey in a large bowl. Add oats and buttermilk. Cover and refrigerate overnight.
2. The next morning mix in beaten eggs.
3. In a separate bowl sift together flour, baking soda and salt. (This also can be done ahead and set aside until morning.)
4. Add dry ingredients to oat mixture.
5. Pour small amounts onto buttered preheated griddle. Gently flip over to cook the second side.

Serve with fresh fruit and maple syrup.

Eggs Brevitato

Serves 6 to 8

A real eye opener!

10 eggs, beaten
4 tablespoons butter, melted
½ teaspoon baking powder
½ teaspoon salt
¼ cup flour
¾ pound Monterey Jack cheese, shredded
8 ounces cottage cheese
1 4-ounce can green chilies,
   drained and chopped

1. Preheat oven to 350°.
2. Grease 13x9x2-inch pan.
3. Combine eggs, butter, baking powder, salt, flour, cheeses and chilies.
4. Pour into pan and bake 40 minutes until top is light brown.

Serve with corn muffins and margaritas. (Yes, for breakfast!)

Smoky Egg Casserole

Serves 6 to 8

What a wonderful way to start, or perhaps, end the day.

2 tablespoons butter
2 tablespoons flour
1¼ cups milk
1 6-ounce package smoked cheese, grated
12 eggs
1 cup cooked peas
6 ounces mushrooms, sliced
1 tablespoon fresh chives, minced
½ cup croutons
6 slices bacon, cooked and crumbled

1. Preheat oven to 350°.
2. In a saucepan melt butter and blend in flour. Gradually stir in milk, stirring constantly.
3. Add cheese and set aside.
4. Beat eggs in a large bowl. Blend in peas, mushrooms and chives.
5. Sauté egg mixture in buttered frypan until set.
6. Stir in cheese sauce.
7. Pour egg mixture into baking dish and bake for 20 minutes.
8. Top with croutons and bacon and bake 10 more minutes.

Omelette Italiano

Serves 2

Italian touches add gusto to this omelet.

1 tablespoon oil
1 Italian plum tomato, chopped
1 cup steamed cauliflower
1 teaspoon basil
4 eggs, beaten
4 tablespoons cold water
½ cup Parmesan cheese, grated

1. In frypan over medium heat, sauté tomato, cauliflower and basil in oil.
2. Add beaten eggs and water.
3. Cook until set. Sprinkle with Parmesan cheese.
4. Fold over and finish cooking.

Serve hot with crusty bread.

Eggs Victorian

Serves 10 to 12

Prepare in the evening, set oven timer to preheat, and pop in the oven when you awaken.

1 pound breakfast sausage links
1 loaf French bread
4 tablespoons flour
2 tablespoons dry mustard
dash of pepper
¼ teaspoon basil
5 cups milk
10 eggs
4 tablespoons butter, melted
1 cup cheddar cheese, grated

Must be made ahead.

1. Place sausage in saucepan, cover with water and boil 3 to 5 minutes; drain and cool.
2. Break bread into small pieces and sprinkle in bottom of greased 9x13-inch pan.
3. Cut up sausage and sprinkle over bread.
4. In a small bowl combine flour, mustard, pepper and basil; sprinkle over sausage.
5. In a separate bowl mix together milk, eggs and butter; pour over above ingredients making sure all are moistened.
6. Sprinkle cheese on top.
7. Cover with aluminum foil and refrigerate overnight.
8. Preheat oven to 350°.
9. Bake covered for 1 hour.

Serve hot with or without maple syrup.

Stuffed French Toast

Serves 6 to 8

To catch a few extra zzzzz's, make this ahead.

8 slices bread, crust removed
   and bread cubed
2 8-ounce packages cream cheese, cubed
12 eggs
2 cups milk
⅓ cup maple syrup

1. Place cubed bread slices and cream cheese in a 9x13-inch lightly greased baking dish. Layer bread first, then cream cheese, then bread.
2. In a large bowl mix together eggs, milk and syrup and pour over bread and cheese cubes.
3. Cover with foil and refrigerate overnight.
4. Preheat oven to 375°.
5. Uncover casserole and bake for 45 minutes until golden.

Serve with warm syrup.

Sausage Apple Bake

Serves 4 to 6

Tell everyone you "slaved" for hours preparing this breakfast and they'll believe you.

8 sausage links (pork or turkey), sliced
6 tart apples, sliced
¾ cup brown sugar
1 cup apple cider
1 package buttermilk biscuits (10)

1. Preheat oven to 400°.
2. Arrange sausages in 8-inch square baking pan.
3. Sprinkle apples, brown sugar and cider on top.
4. Bake for 15 minutes.
5. Lower oven to 350°.
6. Remove pan from oven and layer biscuits on top of sausages and apples. Baste with juices.
7. Bake additional 30 minutes.

Serve hot with maple syrup.

Wake Up Waffles

Serves 4

Club soda makes these luscious waffles extra light.

2 cups buttermilk baking mix
1 egg
½ cup oil
1½ cups club soda

1. Heat waffle maker.
2. In a medium bowl mix buttermilk baking mix, egg, oil and club soda.
3. Bake waffles according to directions on waffle maker.

Serve hot with fresh fruit or syrup.

Patty's Wonderful Waffles

Serves 4

There is nothing ordinary about these waffles.

1¾ cups flour
2 teaspoons baking powder
3 teaspoons sugar
½ teaspoon salt
3 egg yolks, beaten
1½ cups milk
½ cup vegetable oil
3 egg whites, stiffly beaten
1 cup blueberries, fresh or frozen, thawed
blueberry syrup

1. Preheat waffle iron.
2. Measure dry ingredients into a medium bowl.
3. In a separate bowl combine beaten egg yolks with milk and add to dry ingredients.
4. Stir in oil.
5. Fold in egg whites. DO NOT OVERMIX.
6. Pour one cup batter into preheated waffle iron.
7. Close and bake approximately 3 minutes.

Serve hot with blueberries and blueberry syrup.

Brunch Soufflé

Feed your children breakfast in bed!

Serves 6 to 8

1 pound bulk sausage (turkey OR pork)
6 eggs, beaten
2 cups milk
1 teaspoon salt
1 tablespoon dry mustard
6 slices bread, cubed
1 cup cheddar cheese, grated

1. In a medium frypan brown sausage; drain and cool; crumble into a bowl and set aside.
2. In a medium bowl, combine beaten eggs, milk, salt, mustard and bread cubes. Mix well. Stir in cheese and sausage.
3. Pour into greased 12x8x2-inch baking dish.
4. Cover and refrigerate overnight.
5. Next day, preheat oven to 350°.
6. Uncover casserole and bake for 45 minutes until golden on top.

Serve warm with syrup or cream.

Apple Butter Muffins

Makes 12 muffins

2 cups flour
1 tablespoon baking powder
½ teaspoon salt
1 teaspoon cinnamon
⅔ cup sugar
1 egg, beaten
⅓ cup butter, melted
¾ cup milk
½ cup apple butter
1 tablespoon orange rind, grated
1 cup raisins

1. Preheat oven to 400°.
2. In a large bowl stir together flour, baking powder, salt, cinnamon and sugar.
3. Stir in egg, butter, milk and apple butter until moistened.
4. Fold in orange rind and raisins.
5. Fill paper lined muffin tins three-quarters full and bake 20 minutes.
6. When done remove muffins to wire rack to cool.

Serve hot, spread with more apple butter.

Blueberry Puffs

1 cup buttermilk baking mix
1 cup multi-grain pancake mix
    (available at health food stores)
2 eggs
⅔ cup milk
⅓ cup sugar
2 tablespoons butter, melted
1 cup blueberries, fresh
    or frozen, thawed

Makes 12 muffins

1. Preheat oven to 400°.
2. In a medium bowl combine buttermilk baking mix and pancake mix.
3. In a small bowl, beat eggs. Add milk, sugar and melted butter. Mix well and add to dry mixes.
4. Fold in 1 cup blueberries.
5. Bake in greased muffin tin for 15 to 20 minutes.
6. Remove muffins to wire rack to cool.

Serve warm with Lemon Blanket (see index) or lemon marmalade.

Piña Colada Muffins

Will satisfy any sweet tooth.

½ cup sugar
1 egg
¼ cup (½ stick) butter
1 teaspoon rum extract
½ cup plain yogurt
½ cup sour cream
½ cup flaked coconut
1 8-ounce can crushed pineapple,
    drained
1½ cups flour
1 teaspoon baking powder
½ teaspoon salt
½ teaspoon baking soda

Makes 12 muffins

1. Preheat oven to 350°.
2. Grease a 12-cup muffin tin.
3. In a medium bowl cream together sugar, egg, butter and rum extract.
4. Add yogurt, sour cream, coconut and pineapple; mix well.
5. In a separate bowl combine flour, baking powder, salt and baking soda. Add to other ingredients mixing thoroughly.
6. Spoon mixture into muffin cups and bake 15 to 20 minutes.
7. When done, remove muffins to wire rack to cool.

Buttermilk Scones

Makes 8 scones

Bake when you have time to sit quietly and savor the flavor.

2 cups flour
⅓ cup sugar
1½ teaspoons baking powder
½ teaspoon baking soda
¼ teaspoon salt
6 tablespoons unsalted butter, chilled
½ cup buttermilk
I large egg
I teaspoon vanilla
⅔ cup currants or raisins (Optional)

1. Preheat oven to 400°.
2. In a large bowl stir together flour, sugar, baking powder, baking soda and salt.
3. Cut butter into ½-inch cubes and spread over flour mixture.
4. Cut butter into flour mixture with pastry blender until mixture resembles coarse crumbs.
5. In a separate bowl stir together buttermilk, egg and vanilla.
6. Add buttermilk mixture to flour mixture and stir until well blended.
7. Add currants or raisins if desired.
8. Pat the dough into an 8-inch circle on ungreased cookie sheet.
9. With a serrated knife, cut into 8 wedges.
10. Slightly separate wedges from each other.
11. Bake for 15 minutes until lightly browned.

Serve hot with butter and jam.

L.C. Johnson Scones

Makes 8 to 10 scones

***Nothing* can surpass a warm scone for breakfast.**

2 cups flour
I tablespoon baking powder
½ teaspoon salt
6 tablespoons sugar
6 tablespoons butter
2 eggs, beaten
½ cup milk

1. Preheat oven to 425°.
2. In a small bowl mix flour, baking powder, salt and sugar.
3. Cut in butter with a pastry blender until crumbly.
4. Add eggs and milk. Stir until just blended.
5. Drop ¼- to ⅓-cup batter for each scone onto ungreased cookie sheet.
6. Bake 10 minutes until lightly browned..

Serve hot with butter and jam.

Poppy Muffins

1 regular package yellow or white cake mix
1 3-ounce package vanilla
  instant pudding mix
½ cup poppy seeds
4 eggs
1 cup sour cream
½ cup cream sherry
¼ cup oil

Makes 18 muffins

1. Preheat oven to 400°.
2. Grease and flour muffin tins.
3. In a large mixing bowl mix together cake mix, instant pudding, poppy seeds, eggs, sour cream, cream sherry and oil. Beat thoroughly until smooth.
4. Pour into muffin cups.
5. Bake 10 to 15 minutes.
6. Remove muffins to wire rack to cool.

Apple Pillows

1 17-ounce package frozen puff pastry
2 cooking apples
½ cup brown sugar, firmly packed
2 tablespoons flour
1 teaspoon lemon peel, grated
1 teaspoon fresh lemon juice
1 teaspoon cinnamon
½ teaspoon nutmeg, freshly grated
1 large egg, lightly beaten
whipped cream (Optional)

Makes 9 pillows

1. Preheat oven to 375°.
2. Thaw frozen puff pastry according to package instructions.
3. Peel, core and coarsely chop apples to measure about 2 cups.
4. In bowl, toss apples with sugar, flour, lemon peel, lemon juice, cinnamon and nutmeg.
5. On lightly floured surface cut each of 2 pastry sheets into nine 3x3-inch squares.
6. Place scant ¼ cup apple mixture in center of each of nine squares.
7. Brush edges of squares with beaten egg.
8. Top each filled pastry square with second square, press edges with fingers to seal.
9. Decorate borders by pressing gently with tines of a fork.
10. Using sharp knife, make 1-inch L-shaped cut in center of each pie; fold back pastry flaps.
11. Place pies on ungreased cookie sheet; brush with beaten egg.
12. Bake 20 minutes until golden.
13. Remove "pillows" to wire rack to cool.

Serve warm or at room temperature, with whipped cream, if desired.

Lena's World Famous Grapenut Pudding   Serves 10

Homespun and hearty.

4 cups milk
1 teaspoon butter
1 cup grapenuts
2 eggs, well beaten
½ cup sugar
½ teaspoon salt
1 teaspoon vanilla

1. Preheat oven to 325°.
2. In a medium saucepan heat milk and butter until butter melts.
3. Remove from heat and add grapenuts. Let stand for 10 minutes.
4. Stir in eggs, sugar, salt and vanilla.
5. Pour mixture into 10 greased custard cups.
6. Put cups into a baking pan filled with 1½-inches of water.
7. Bake for 45 minutes.
8. Remove from water and cool on rack.

Serve warm or cold with cream or syrup.

Cozy Quilt Compote   Serves 6

Sensational on waffles, French toast, pancakes, omelettes, soufflés, chocolate cake, pound cake, ice cream, yogurt, etc., etc., etc.

3 oranges, pared and sectioned
3 bananas, sliced
1 pint fresh strawberries, halved
¼ cup coffee flavored liqueur
1 tablespoon cinnamon

1. Combine fruit in a small bowl.
2. Pour liqueur over fruit, stir and chill.
3. Before serving blend in cinnamon.

Lemon Blanket

Similar to English lemon curd.

Makes 2 cups

1 rounded tablespoon flour
1 pound sugar
3 small lemons, juiced
1 tablespoon butter
3 eggs

1. In a small bowl mix together flour and sugar; set aside.
2. In a double boiler over low heat, mix together the juice of 3 lemons, butter, and eggs.
3. Slowly add dry ingredients, stirring constantly.
4. Cook over medium heat stirring occasionally until mixture becomes thick, like pudding.
5. Pour into sterilized jars, cover and refrigerate.

Serve cold on biscuits, scones or muffins.

Lullabies

And goodnight.

Serves 2

1 16-ounce can pineapple-grapefruit juice
3 ounces bourbon
crushed ice

1. Combine juice and bourbon.
2. Fill two glasses half full of crushed ice.
3. Pour juice mixture over ice and serve.

ON THE ROAD

SAMPLE MENU

Nippy Garlic Pecans

Red Foliage Pepper Soup

Fall's Perfect Pizza Bread

Hot October Cranberry Tea

Glazed Autumn Apple Cookies

Crisp Red Apples

Often our adventures take us on road trips. Highways may carry us to distant destinations, or simply provide an afternoon's or even an hour's escape from the familiar setting. Plan a meal or snack that can be packed quickly and taken along. You may discover a lakeside park, a scenic overlook or a beckoning meadow for your picnic. If not, set the hood or trunk of your car as an attractive table when you stop. If time is limited, or hunger pangs plead to be quelled, you may even eat en route. Whatever the dining situation, you really "auto" try some of the recipes in this section for your trips "on the road."

Nippy Garlic Pecans

Makes 2 cups

Always have these on hand. They will keep forever!

¼ cup (½ stick) butter, melted
½ teaspoon Tabasco sauce
1 teaspoon Worcestershire sauce
1 tablespoon garlic powder
⅛ teaspoon salt
2 cups shelled pecans

1. Preheat oven to 300°.
2. Mix all ingredients except pecans thoroughly.
3. Add pecans and stir gently to coat the nuts.
4. Spread coated pecans on cookie sheet.
5. Bake at 300° for 30 minutes.
6. Drain on paper towels. Cool and refrigerate.

Red Foliage Pepper Soup

Serves 6

3 large red peppers, coarsely chopped
2 cups leeks, coarsely chopped
1 tablespoon butter
2 tablespoons safflower oil
1 cup double strength chicken broth, defatted
3 cups buttermilk
2 tablespoons soy sauce
½ teaspoon black pepper, freshly ground

1. In a large stockpot sauté peppers and leeks in butter and oil for 15 minutes.
2. Add broth and simmer partially covered for 30 minutes.
3. Cool. Blend in food processor and strain.
4. Stir in buttermilk.
5. Add soy sauce and pepper.
6. Strain again.

This soup freezes well and can be served hot or cold.

For a special meal at home — serve in hollowed-out green, yellow or purple pepper and garnish with a thin slice of lime.

Creamy Iced Tomato Soup

Serves 4 to 6

2 large ripe tomatoes, peeled and diced
1 clove garlic, crushed
1 teaspoon sugar
1 tablespoon salt
½ teaspoon pepper
2 cups tomato juice
1 cup sour cream
1 large cucumber, thinly sliced

1. In a large bowl mix together tomatoes, garlic, sugar, salt, pepper and tomato juice.
2. Cover and refrigerate overnight.
3. When ready to serve, add sour cream and cucumber.

Spicy Italian Sandwich

1 4-ounce jar marinated artichoke hearts
1 clove garlic, crushed
1 4-ounce jar roasted red peppers, drained
½ cup green olives
¼ cup olive oil
1 loaf French bread
⅛ pound Mozzarella cheese
⅛ pound Provolone cheese
¼ pound Italian cold cuts

Serves 4 to 6

1. Combine artichokes with marinade, garlic, pepper, green olives, and olive oil in food processor and process until well blended.
2. Split bread lengthwise and spread mixture on both sides of bread.
3. Layer selection of Italian cheeses and meats on bread.
4. Slice and serve.

Reuben-Wich

3¼ cups flour
1 tablespoon sugar
1 teaspoon salt
1 package rapid-rise yeast
1 cup hot water
1 tablespoon butter
¼ cup Thousand Island dressing
½ pound corned beef, thinly sliced
¼ pound Swiss cheese, thinly sliced
1 8-ounce can sauerkraut, well drained
1 egg white, beaten
1 teaspoon caraway seed

Makes 1 large loaf

1. Preheat oven to 400°.
2. Set aside 1 cup flour. In large bowl, mix remaining flour, sugar, salt and yeast.
3. Stir in hot water and butter. Mix well.
4. Mix in only enough reserved flour to make soft dough.
5. On floured surface, knead 5 minutes.
6. On greased baking sheet, roll dough to 10x14-inches.
7. Spread dressing down center third of dough.
8. Top dressing with layers of beef, cheese and sauerkraut.
9. Make cuts from filling to dough edges at 1-inch intervals along sides of filling.
10. Alternating sides, fold strips at an angle across filling; cover with a clean cloth.
11. Place large shallow pan half filled with boiling water on counter.
12. Place baking sheet over pan; let dough rise 15 minutes.
13. Brush with egg white; sprinkle with caraway seed.
14. Bake for 25 minutes or until lightly browned.
15. Cool slightly; slice and serve warm.
16. Refrigerate leftovers; reheat to serve.

Oven Crisp Chicken

Serves 4

Children like to shake the chicken in the bag.

¼ cup flour
1 teaspoon paprika
¼ teaspoon salt
½ teaspoon crushed red pepper
½ teaspoon black pepper
3 pounds chicken parts, skin removed
1 tablespoon butter, melted

1. Preheat oven to 375°.
2. Place dry ingredients in brown paper bag or large self-locking bag.
3. Roll chicken in melted butter.
4. Toss chicken in bag with dry ingredients.
5. Bake in a shallow baking pan for 50 minutes.

Serve hot or cold; not greasy; packs well.

Fall's Perfect Pizza Bread

Makes 1 large loaf

2½ cups all purpose flour
½ teaspoon salt
¾ teaspoon dry yeast
1 cup warm water
2 tablespoons olive oil
½ teaspoon garlic powder
½ teaspoon rosemary leaves
½ cup EACH shredded Mozzarella,
    Fontina and Parmesan cheese
1 8-ounce pepperoni stick, sliced

1. Combine flour, salt, yeast and water in a bowl. Blend well.
2. Knead dough on floured board. Shape into a ball. Place in a greased bowl. Cover with towel. Let rise for one hour.
3. Punch dough down. Cover and let rise one more hour.
4. Preheat oven to 350°.
5. Roll out dough to ½-inch thickness. Brush 1½ tablespoons olive oil over the dough and sprinkle with garlic powder and rosemary leaves.
6. Cover surface of dough with shredded cheeses and pepperoni slices. Press pepperoni into dough.
7. Roll up dough jellyroll fashion. Tuck in seams and place on cookie sheet, seam side down.
8. Brush top with ½ tablespoon olive oil.
9. Bake for 25 to 30 minutes.
10. Let cool in pan 10 minutes before slicing.

Serve warm or cold.
Freezes well, before or after baking.

Pumpkin Loaf

Makes 1 loaf

1 teaspoon cinnamon
2 cups sugar
2½ cups flour
½ teaspoon salt
½ teaspoon baking powder
1 teaspoon baking soda
3 eggs
2 cups canned pumpkin OR squash
1 cup (2 sticks) butter, melted

1. Preheat oven to 325°.
2. Mix dry ingredients together in large bowl.
3. Add eggs, pumpkin and butter. Stir until well blended.
4. Bake for 1 hour in a greased 9x5x3-inch loaf pan.
5. Cool in pan 5 minutes. Remove bread to wire rack to complete cooling.

Raspberry Tart

Makes 18 tarts

1½ cups flour
1 cup (2 sticks) butter
½ cup sour cream
raspberry preserves

Sugar Glaze:
1 tablespoon water
3 tablespoons sugar

Requires some advance preparation.

1. Mix flour, butter and sour cream to make dough.
2. Refrigerate overnight.
3. Preheat oven to 350°.
4. Divide refrigerated dough in half to ease in rolling.
5. Roll dough on a floured board to ⅛-inch thick.
6. Cut out 36 2½-inch circles. Cut a 1-inch circle from the center of 18 of the circles.
7. Place whole circles on ungreased cookie sheet. Top with remaining circles.
8. Brush on Sugar Glaze.
9. Fill centers with raspberry preserves, about ½ to 1 teaspoon each.
10. Bake for 25 minutes until lightly browned.
11. Rotate cookie sheets to promote even browning.
12. Cool tarts on racks.

Chocolate Pound Cake

Cake:

5 squares unsweetened chocolate
1⅓ cups water
2 cups flour
2 cups sugar
1 teaspoon salt
½ cup (1 stick) butter
3 eggs
1 teaspoon aromatic bitters
1 teaspoon vanilla
2 teaspoons baking powder

Cake preparation:

1. In a small saucepan combine chocolate and water. Heat, stirring constantly, until chocolate melts; cool until lukewarm.
2. Sift flour, sugar and salt into a large mixing bowl. Cut in butter with a pastry blender to make a crumbly mixture.
3. Add cooled chocolate mixture. Beat at medium speed for 5 minutes. Chill batter in bowl for 1 hour.
4. Preheat oven to 300°.
5. Return bowl to mixer. Beat at medium speed 1 minute. Add eggs, one at a time, beating 1 minute after each addition. Add aromatic bitters and vanilla and beat 2 minutes. Add baking powder and beat 2 minutes more.
6. Pour batter into a greased 8-cup bundt pan (or a 9x5x3-inch loaf pan) which has been lightly dusted with dry cocoa.
7. Bake in oven for 1¾ hours or until a toothpick inserted in center comes out clean. Cool pan on wire rack 10 minutes; loosen around edges with a knife. Turn cake out of pan on a wire rack and cool completely.
8. Frost with Chocolate Glaze and garnish with sliced almonds or chopped walnuts.

Chocolate Glaze:

1 4-ounce package sweet chocolate
1 tablespoon butter
3 tablespoons water
1 cup confectioner's sugar
dash of salt
1 teaspoon vanilla

Chocolate Glaze preparation:

1. Break chocolate pieces into a medium saucepan. Heat with butter and water, stirring constantly, until chocolate melts.
2. Remove from heat; beat in sugar and salt until smooth; stir in vanilla.
3. Let cool 5 minutes, stirring to keep glaze from hardening.
4. Pour on cooled chocolate pound cake. Sprinkle with nuts.

Glaze hardens on this dense cake, which makes it easy to cut, wrap and travel.

Glazed Autumn Apple Cookies   Makes 4½ dozen cookies

Leaf peeping munchables.

4½ cups flour
2 teaspoons baking soda
1 teaspoon salt
1 teaspoon cloves
1 teaspoon nutmeg
2 teaspoons cinnamon
1 cup butter (2 sticks)
2⅔ cups brown sugar, packed
2 eggs
1 cup cider
2 cups apples (Ida Red or Jonathan),
    unpeeled and shredded
1 cup raisins
1½ cups nuts, chopped

1. Preheat oven to 375°.
2. In small bowl, sift together flour, baking soda, salt and spices.
3. In large bowl, cream butter and brown sugar.
4. Add eggs, cider and apples. Mix well.
5. Add dry ingredients, raisins and nuts. Mix thoroughly.
6. Drop from tablespoon onto greased cookie sheet.
7. Bake for 10 minutes.
8. Glaze while hot and remove from pan to cool.

Glaze:

1 tablespoon butter
1½ cups confectioner's sugar
⅛ teaspoon salt
3½ teaspoons cider*
½ teaspoon vanilla

Glaze preparation:

1. In a large bowl cream butter, sugar and salt.
2. Stir in cider and vanilla. Mix well.
3. Glaze cookies while hot.

***Orange juice or milk can be substituted for cider.
Don't use vanilla when using orange juice.**

Hot October Cranberry Tea   Makes 6 quarts

Conjures up memories of mild autumn days when served warm or over ice.

1½ quarts cranberry juice
1 cup sugar
3 quarts water
12 whole cloves
1 cinnamon stick
1 12-ounce can frozen orange juice
    concentrate plus 1 juice can of water
1 12-ounce can frozen lemonade
    concentrate plus 1 juice can of water
2 cups pineapple juice

1. Combine cranberry juice, sugar and 1 quart of water with spices.
2. Simmer 20 minutes.
3. Add remaining 2 quarts of water plus other ingredients and heat thoroughly, but do not boil.
4. Serve immediately or freeze in quart portions. Thaw and heat as needed.

BIRD
WATCHING

SAMPLE MENU

Seedeater Granola

Devil-Down-Headed Eggs

Yellow Bird

Cardinal Soup

Sage And Cheddar Quackers

Pigeon Pea Pasta Salad

Squab-Ke-Babs

Baltimore Oriole Cake

Pineapple Audubon-Bons

"Is that a sulphur-bellied flycatcher perched on a fork-leafed toothwart?" Sometimes bird watchers seem to have their own language as they stalk their feathered friends with focused binoculars and abundant enthusiasm. What fun for the whole family or a large group of friends! To keep the energy level high (so feathers don't get ruffled) try our delicious sample menu. Or you might want to "wing it" and mix and match the delectable recipes in this section to enhance your adventure of peering and peeking.

Devil-Down-Headed Eggs

Serves 6 to 8

Use egg carton not only to store eggs, but also as a serving container.

12 hard-boiled eggs
3 tablespoons mayonnaise
1 tablespoon chutney, finely chopped
½ teaspoon curry powder
¼ teaspoon salt
⅛ teaspoon pepper
1 tablespoon walnuts, finely chopped
1 teaspoon flaked coconut
   plus additional coconut for garnish

1. Standing eggs upright, cut pointed ends horizontally and remove yolks.
2. Mash yolks and mix with remaining ingredients.
3. With pastry bag or spoon, fill eggs with mixture and stand in egg carton.
4. Sprinkle with additional coconut.
5. Close carton cover and eggs are ready to travel.

Seedeater Granola

Makes 2 quarts

This nutty treat is great plain, with yogurt, or over ice cream.

1 cup wheat germ
1 cup unsweetened flaked coconut
4 cups regular oatmeal (not instant)
¼ cup sesame seeds
½ cup sunflower seeds
1 cup raw almonds
1 cup raw cashews
½ cup honey
⅔ cup corn oil
1 teaspoon vanilla
¼ teaspoon salt
½ cup dates, chopped
½ cup dried apricots, chopped
½ cup dried cherries, chopped
½ cup raisins

1. Preheat oven to 300°.
2. Combine first seven ingredients in a large bowl and mix together.
3. Combine honey, corn oil, vanilla and salt in a saucepan. Cook over low heat until honey is melted.
4. Pour over the dry mixture and blend thoroughly.
5. Spread in a greased jellyroll pan and bake for 35 to 45 minutes. STIR every 10 minutes during baking.
6. Remove and cool.
7. Add dried fruits, mix and store in airtight container.

Can be served in a small, CLEAN, open birdfeeder.

24

Sage and Cheddar Quackers

Makes 2 dozen

Wonderful flavor served with soup or as an hors d'oeuvre.

¾ cup flour
¼ teaspoon salt
dash of cayenne pepper
1 rounded teaspoon sage
¼ cup pecans, finely ground
⅓ cup butter
1 cup extra sharp cheddar cheese, grated

1. Preheat oven to 350°.
2. Sift flour, salt, pepper and sage together.
3. Place in bowl of food processor with ground pecans. Mix until blended.
4. With motor running, drop in chunks of butter and then the cheese, processing until the dough forms a ball.
5. Roll out on a slightly floured board to ¼-inch thickness.
6. Cut in bird shapes and bake on ungreased cookie sheet 10 to 12 minutes until the edges turn golden brown.
7. Cool on rack and then place in airtight container to store.

Pigeon Pea Pasta Salad

Serves 8 to 10

Substitute other beans such as chick peas or fava beans.

2 16-ounce cans pigeon peas
1 clove garlic, crushed
½ cup pitted black olives, halved
⅓ cup red onion, chopped
⅓ cup fresh parsley, chopped
¼ cup wine vinegar
1 teaspoon salt
½ teaspoon pepper
½ cup olive oil
1 pound cooked pasta

Choose interesting pasta shapes such as shells or wheels. Also try different flavors such as spinach, carrot or beet.

1. Drain pigeon peas and rinse.
2. In a bowl, mix peas, garlic, olives, onion and parsley.
3. In small jar, shake together vinegar, salt and pepper until salt dissolves. Add oil and shake again to combine.
4. Pour dressing over pigeon pea and pasta mixture and toss all together.

Serve at room temperature.

Pea-Nutty Salad

Serves 6 to 8

1 1-pound package frozen peas, thawed
1 cup peanuts
½ cup celery, sliced
½ cup onion, sliced
½ cup carrots, shredded
½ pound bacon, cooked and crumbled

Dressing:
½ cup mayonnaise
½ cup sour cream
2 teaspoons Worcestershire sauce

1. Combine peas, peanuts, celery, onion, carrots and bacon in large bowl.
2. Stir together mayonnaise, sour cream and Worcestershire sauce in medium bowl.
3. Pour dressing over salad ingredients and toss.

Can be added to 2 cups cooked pasta or 2 cups cooked rice.

Tuna Pasta Salad

Serves 8 to 10

This is a "toss everything from the fridge and pantry into this salad" salad.

2 cups elbow macaroni
2 small cans tuna, drained and flaked
2 eggs, hard-boiled and chopped
2 tomatoes, chopped
½ cup celery, diced
½ cup onion, diced
4 strips bacon, cooked and crumbled
6 sweet gherkin pickles, diced
½ cup cheddar cheese, diced
¾ cup light mayonnaise
½ cup sour cream OR yogurt
pickle juice
½ teaspoon garlic powder
½ teaspoon salt
¼ teaspoon pepper

You may add or substitute ham, Spanish olives, green bean pieces, fresh peas or diced American cheese.

1. Cook macaroni according to package directions.
2. Combine macaroni, tuna, eggs, tomatoes, celery, onion, bacon, pickles and cheese in a large bowl.
3. In a separate bowl combine mayonnaise, sour cream and a small amount of pickle juice.
4. To this add garlic powder, salt and pepper.
5. Mix thoroughly into pasta mixture and chill several hours before serving.

Cardinal Soup

Serves 6

3 cans tomato soup or tomato bisque
2 cups milk
1 cup cream or half-and-half
1 tablespoon Worcestershire sauce
1 tablespoon horseradish

1. In a large saucepan mix all ingredients together and heat to boiling.
2. Place in thermos and keep warm until ready to serve.

Mugs would be the perfect picnic vessels and any cracker might do, but Sage & Cheddar Quackers (see index) would be ideal!

Squab-Ke-Babs

Serves 8

If you cannot find squab, try quail or cornish game hens.

4 squabs (½ squab per person)
Corn on-the-cob, cut in 2-inch pieces
    (1 piece for each serving)
Red and green peppers, cut in 2-inch squares
    (1 piece for each serving)
8 new potatoes, half cooked
8 large mushrooms
8 pieces zucchini, yellow or
    patty pan squash

Marinade:

1½ cups olive oil
½ cup lemon juice
6 cloves garlic, crushed
1 tablespoon rosemary, ground
1 teaspoon salt
½ teaspoon pepper

1. Remove backbones from all birds and open each one, flattening it with palm of hand.
2. Slice each bird in half.
3. Prepare marinade by mixing all marinade ingredients.
4. Marinate squab and vegetables in refrigerator 6 to 8 hours or overnight.
5. Drain marinade and skewer birds and vegetables separately. (When skewering birds, be sure to poke skewer up and down through meat for a tight hold.)
6. Grill birds and vegetables 5 minutes on each side being sure fire is not too hot nor food too close to flame.
7. Remove food from skewers when done and serve on turkey platter.

Lemon Rice

¼ cup (½ stick) butter
½ teaspoon salt
½ teaspoon mustard seed
½ teaspoon ground turmeric
1½ cups quick cooking rice
1½ cups water
1 tablespoon lemon juice

1. In medium saucepan melt butter over low heat.
2. Stir in salt, mustard seed and turmeric. Cook for 5 minutes, stirring occasionally.
3. Stir in quick cooking rice, water and lemon juice. Bring to boiling; reduce heat and simmer, covered, about 5 minutes or until rice is tender.

Serve hot or cold.

Orange Rolls

Better double this recipe since they'll be *flocking* for more than one.

Rolls:
1 package dry yeast
1 cup warm water
3 tablespoons sugar
2 tablespoons butter, melted
1 egg
¾ teaspoon salt
3 to 3½ cups flour
¼ cup butter, softened
2 tablespoons sugar
2 tablespoons orange rind, grated

1. In a large mixing bowl dissolve yeast in warm water with a pinch of sugar (from the 3 tablespoons of sugar). When frothy add sugar, butter, egg, salt and half the flour.
2. Beat on low speed with mixer until smooth.
3. Stir in enough of the remaining flour to make a soft dough. Put in a large, greased bowl, turn dough to grease all sides. Cover and let rise 1 hour or until doubled in size.
4. Punch dough down and turn out onto a floured surface.
5. Roll into a rectangular shape approximately 9x14-inches.
6. Combine softened butter, the 2 tablespoons of sugar, and orange rind in a bowl. Spread on dough.
7. Roll from 14-inch side, jellyroll-style and cut into 9 1½-inch thick slices.
8. Place slices into greased 9-inch cake pan. Cover and let rise 1 hour or until doubled in size.

9. Preheat oven to 350° and bake 25 to 30 minutes.
10. Pour Glaze over rolls as soon as they come out of the oven.

Glaze:

½ cup sugar
¼ cup (½ stick) butter
¼ cup sour cream
1 tablespoon orange juice

Glaze preparation:

1. Combine sugar, butter, sour cream and juice in a small saucepan.
2. Cook over low heat until heated thoroughly, stirring constantly.

Rolls can be frozen without the glaze. Reheat and glaze before serving.

Baltimore Oriole Cake

Serves 10 to 12

This cake is very moist, yet firm. Will "travel" well, even if precut.

1 cup (2 sticks) butter
2 cups sugar
½ teaspoon vanilla
2 tablespoons orange rind
5 eggs
3 cups flour
1 tablespoon baking powder
pinch salt
¾ cup milk

1. Preheat oven to 350°.
2. In a large bowl cream together butter and sugar until fluffy.
3. Add vanilla and orange rind and mix thoroughly.
4. Add eggs, one at a time, beating after each addition.
5. Sift twice, flour, baking powder and salt and add to creamed mixture a little at a time alternately with milk. Beat well.
6. Pour batter into greased and floured angelfood pan and bake for 1 hour.
7. When cake is a golden color, remove from oven and poke holes all over. Drizzle with Glaze.

Glaze:

¼ cup butter (½ stick)
⅔ cup sugar
⅓ cup orange juice

Glaze preparation:

1. Heat all ingredients in saucepan and pour over cake in pan while cake is still hot.
8. Let cake cool completely before removing from pan.

Pineapple Audubon-Bons

Makes 2 dozen

2 cups flour, sifted
1½ teaspoons baking powder
¼ teaspoon baking soda
¼ teaspoon salt
½ cup (½ stick) butter
1 cup light brown sugar, firmly packed
1 egg
1 teaspoon vanilla
1 8-ounce can crushed pineapple, drained, reserving liquid for glaze

Use a 2 tablespoon scoop to keep a uniform ☞ "bon-bon" shape.

1. Preheat oven to 400°.
2. Sift flour with baking powder, baking soda and salt. Set aside.
3. In large bowl, cream butter with sugar until light.
4. Beat in egg and vanilla until light and fluffy.
5. Add drained pineapple and mix well.
6. Stir in flour mixture until well combined.
7. Drop by rounded tablespoonfuls, 2 inches apart, onto greased cookie sheet. Bake for 8 to 10 minutes, until golden brown.
8. Remove to wire rack and cool slightly.

Glaze:

4 cups confectioner's sugar, sifted
3 to 4 tablespoons pineapple liquid

Glaze preparation:

1. Combine and stir both glaze ingredients until smooth.
2. Place wax paper under cooling rack to catch drips.
3. Spread glaze on top of warm cookies and let sit until glaze dries and hardens.

Store in an airtight container. The flavor of this cookie increases the day after baking.

Cream Cheese Tarts

Makes 12 tarts

Serve afternoon tea with panache.

2 8-ounce packages cream cheese
2 eggs
¾ cup sugar
1 teaspoon vanilla
12 vanilla wafers
toppings (suggested)
   2 peaches, sliced
   6 strawberries, halved
   36 grapes, halved
   OR canned cherry pie filling.
12 paper baking cups

1. Preheat oven to 350°.
2. In large bowl cream together cream cheese, eggs, sugar and vanilla.
3. In muffin pan, place paper baking cups.
4. Into paper cups place vanilla wafers.
5. On top of each wafer pour cream cheese filling (three-quarters full).
6. Bake 20 minutes.
7. When cooled, top with fresh fruit or canned pie filling.

Petite Sponge Cakes

Makes 6 individual servings

As delicate and impressive as a Robin's egg.

6 eggs
1 cup sugar
1 cup flour
½ teaspoon lemon rind, grated
fresh fruit (optional)
whipped cream (optional)
melted chocolate (optional

1. Preheat oven to 375°.
2. Beat eggs with sugar until light and airy.
3. Add flour and lemon.
4. Bake in greased and floured mini Bundt pans or custard cups for 20 minutes.
5. Cool in pans on wire rack, 5 minutes.
6. Invert pans on wire rack and let cakes continue to cool.

Optional: Place each cake on a separate dessert plate. Top with fresh fruit, whipped cream and drizzle with melted chocolate.

Shish Kebab Marinade

Makes 1 cup

Marinade for 1½ pounds of meat (beef, chicken, lamb,...)

½ cup ketchup
1 teaspoon salt
2 tablespoons beef steak sauce
2 tablespoons sugar
2 tablespoons cider vinegar
2 tablespoons Worcestershire sauce
¼ cup water
2 tablespoons salad oil

1. In a small saucepan heat ketchup, salt, steak sauce, sugar, vinegar, Worcestershire sauce, water and salad oil to boiling.
2. Pour over meat and marinate overnight.
3. Heat again to baste.

Yellow Bird

Makes 6 8-ounce servings

Sip slowly or you may find yourself flying.

2 cups orange juice
2 cups pineapple juice
1½ cups light rum
1 cup Galliano liqueur
¼ cup Creme de Banana liqueur
pineapple cubes, orange slices and
    maraschino cherries as garnish

1. Combine liquids and shake well.
2. Pour into tall ice-filled glasses and serve with a straw.
3. Skewer pineapple cubes, orange slices and maraschino cherries for garnish.

DECK & ROOFTOP GATHERINGS

SAMPLE MENU

Rainbow Punch

Cheese In A Cloud

High Flying Filet

Lemon Bubbles

Tracy's Tip Top Potatoes

Lofty Legumes

Pie In The Sky

Nothing is as uplifting as a change of scene. While Nice is nice, the Grand Canyon is grand and Mystic Seaport is best of all, it is not always possible to escape to such destinations. Nor is it always necessary. A rooftop, a deck, an attic or even a basement can provide a wonderful get away. Just be sure to pack a positive attitude, an amiable assortment of friends and some of our mouth-watering delights. Our sensory sensations will take you miles away and give you a lift . . . even if you can't get to a rooftop!

Cheese In A Cloud

Heavenly.

Serves 8 to 10

1 5-inch wheel of Brie cheese
2 tablespoons honey mustard
¼ cup slivered almonds
1 round loaf of sourdough bread

1. Preheat oven to 350°.
2. Cut a circle of rind from the top of a wheel of Brie cheese, leaving a 1-inch border.
3. Spread honey mustard smoothly on top of the exposed cheese. Top mustard with the slivered almonds evenly spread.
4. Cut a circle in the center of sourdough bread, the size of the wheel of Brie, leaving a 2-inch border. Cut excess bread into cubes.
5. Place Brie inside center of bread cutout and bake for 15 minutes.

To serve: Have guests spread Brie cheese on bread cubes with a knife.

Mandarin Orange Salad

Serves 8 to 10

¼ cup almonds, sliced
4 teaspoons sugar
2 heads of different kinds of lettuce, in bite size pieces
2 stalks celery, chopped
1 11-ounce can mandarin oranges, drained
¼ cup oil
2 tablespoons white vinegar
2 tablespoons sugar

Hint: Transport in a plastic bag. Add dressing just prior to serving.

1. In a small frypan, cook almonds and 4 teaspoons sugar over low heat stirring constantly until sugar is melted and almonds are coated. Break apart when cool.
2. In a large bowl combine lettuce, celery and mandarin oranges.
3. In a separate bowl beat together oil, vinegar and the 2 tablespoons sugar.
4. Put salad ingredients into a large self-locking bag. Add dressing and shake until thoroughly coated.
5. Return to salad bowl.
6. Top with toasted almonds just before serving.

Warm Spinach And Basil Salad   Serves 4 to 6

6 cups fresh spinach
1 cup fresh basil, shredded
½ cup olive oil
3 cloves garlic, crushed
½ cup pine nuts
4 ounces prosciutini, diced
½ teaspoon salt
¼ teaspoon pepper

1. Wash and dry spinach.
2. Toss spinach and basil in a salad bowl.
3. In a saucepan heat olive oil over medium heat. Add garlic and pine nuts and sauté until slightly brown.
4. Add prosciutini and cook 1 more minute.
5. Pour over greens and mix thoroughly.
6. Add salt and pepper and serve immediately.

Curried Lima Bean Soup   Serves 4 to 6

Will spice up those special get-togethers.

1 10-ounce package frozen baby
   lima beans, thawed
2 tablespoons butter
⅓ cup scallions, sliced
1 teaspoon curry powder
½ teaspoon salt
⅛ teaspoon pepper
½ teaspoon dry tarragon
4 sprigs fresh parsley
½ cup light cream
1 13¼-ounce can chicken broth
chopped chives for garnish

1. In medium frypan cook lima beans with butter, scallions, and curry powder until beans are soft. Cool slightly.
2. Empty cooked beans into container of food processor; add salt, pepper, dry tarragon, parsley and cream.
3. Cover and blend at low speed. As soon as blades have reached full momentum, switch to high speed and blend for 20 seconds or until smooth.
4. Pour into double boiler and add chicken broth.
5. Heat over simmering water.
6. Serve each portion garnished with chopped chives.

Three Pepper Chicken with Pasta   Serves 4 to 6

An elegant and colorful summer dinner.

Chicken and pasta:
2 tablespoons olive oil
2 cloves garlic, crushed
½ onion, chopped
1 large green pepper, julienne
1 large red pepper, julienne
1 large yellow pepper, julienne
1 28-ounce can plum tomatoes,
    drained and chopped
1 pound package angel hair pasta
¼ cup prepared pesto sauce
3 large boneless chicken breasts,
    cut in half

Pesto:
2 cups fresh basil
½ cup olive oil
3 tablespoons butter
2 tablespoons Romano cheese
2 tablespoons pine nuts
1 teaspoon salt
¼ pound Parmesan cheese, grated
2 cloves garlic

1. Heat oil in a large, heavy frypan.
2. Add garlic and onion. Sauté until transparent.
3. Add peppers and sauté until soft.
4. Stir in tomatoes. Simmer until just bubbling. Remove from heat.
5. Cook pasta according to package directions. Rinse with cold water. Then mix with prepared Pesto. (See below).
6. Cook chicken on grill, 5 minutes on each side. If time is limited, cook in frypan after removing peppers. Add 1 tablespoon of olive oil and cook 4 to 5 minutes; will pick up flavors of the peppers from frypan.

Pesto preparation:
1. Put all ingredients in food processor and process until a paste forms.
2. When ready to eat add a small amount of water to pesto and heat.
3. Add to hot pasta.

Freeze in ¼-cup portions with a layer of oil on top of each.

Assembly:
1. Place angel hair pasta with pesto sauce on platter.
2. Cut chicken into thin slices and fan on top of pasta.
3. Spoon pepper mixture over chicken.

Can be served hot or cold.

Brazilian Pork

Serves 4 to 6

You don't have to speak Portuguese to love this dish.

½ cup oil
4 teaspoons cumin
½ teaspoon turmeric
2 cloves garlic, crushed
1 teaspoon Worcestershire sauce
1½ pounds pork tenderloin
2 medium onions, sliced
2 limes

1. Combine oil, cumin, turmeric, garlic and Worcestershire sauce in shallow marinating dish.
2. Trim any fat off the pork and cut into 1- to 2-inch cubes. Place in marinade.
3. Cover pork and marinate overnight in the refrigerator or for several hours at room temperature.
4. Preheat broiler.
5. Arange pork on broiler pan and broil close to heat source for approximately 4 to 5 minutes.
6. Turn pork over and add onion slices. Broil an additional 4 minutes, or until done.
7. Serve the pork and onions in a serving dish moistened with some of the marinade and wedges of lime. Squeeze some lime juice over the pork and onions.

Serve with rice.

Daube Provençal French Stew

Serves 10 to 12

No browning necessary.

4 pounds lean beef, cubed
2 medium onions, chopped
1 pound carrots, sliced
½ pound mushrooms, sliced
1 16-ounce can stewed tomatoes, with juice
4 cloves garlic, crushed
½ cup parsley, minced
½ cup pitted black olives, sliced
2 teaspoons salt
1 teaspoon pepper
½ teaspoon thyme
2 bay leaves
1 cup water
dry white wine to cover

Must be made ahead.

1. In a large casserole mix together all ingredients except the water and wine. Add 1 cup water plus enough wine to cover.
2. Cover and let marinate overnight in refrigerator.
3. The next day, cook the covered casserole in a 350° oven for 2½ hours.

Remove bay leaves before serving.
Sauce is thin, but may be thickened with cornstarch. Serve with rice or noodles.

Country Shrimp Pizza

8 ounces frozen bread dough, thawed
3 tablespoons horseradish
½ cup Ricotta cheese
½ pound cooked shrimp
1 teaspoon chives
1 tablespoon scallions, chopped
3 strips bacon, cooked and crumbled
1 teaspoon cracked white pepper
½ cup Mozzarella cheese, shredded
¼ cup Parmesan cheese, grated

Serves 4 to 6

1. Preheat oven to 425°.
2. Spread dough into a 12-inch oiled pizza pan.
3. Mix horseradish and Ricotta cheese and spread over dough.
4. Place shrimp over this.
5. Sprinkle on the remaining ingredients.
6. Bake for 15 to 20 minutes or until golden brown.

High Flying Filet

1 whole beef filet, about 4 pounds
1 tablespoon seasoned salt
1 tablespoon black pepper
1 tablespoon meat tenderizer*
1 tablespoon soy sauce

* Omit meat tenderizer if you are sensitive to MSG.

Serves 8 to 10

1. Form a paste with salt, pepper, meat tenterizer and soy sauce. Spread on beef.
2. Place beef on heavy foil and broil 10 minutes on each side.
3. Reduce oven to 350°.
4. Seal filet in foil and bake 20 minutes.
5. Remove from oven and open foil so meat does not continue to bake.
6. Slice and serve with Sour Cream Sauce.

Sour Cream Sauce:
1 cup sour cream
2 tablespoons Dijon mustard
1 teaspoon horseradish

Sauce preparation:

1. Mix together sour cream, mustard and horseradish in a small bowl.
2. Refrigerate until ready to serve.

Lofty Legumes

2 pounds fresh green beans
¾ cup chives
1 small bunch fresh dill
4 tablespoons fresh parsley
3 tablespoons cider vinegar
½ cup walnuts
½ cup olive oil
½ teaspoon salt
¼ teaspoon pepper

Serves 6 to 8

1. Steam green beans, drain and let cool slightly.
2. In a food processor blend chives, dill, parsley, vinegar, walnuts, olive oil, salt and pepper.
3. Process until smooth adding more oil if necessary.
4. Pour over warm beans and chill 1 to 2 hours.

Serve at room temperature.

Tracy's Tip Top Potatoes

Serves 12

Make enough for second helpings.

2 pounds frozen hash brown potatoes,
   thawed for 30 minutes
½ cup (1 stick) butter, melted
2 cups sharp cheddar cheese, grated
1 pint sour cream
1 can cream of chicken soup
1 cup onions, diced
1 teaspoon salt
½ teaspoon pepper
½ cup potato chips, crushed

1. Preheat oven to 375°.
2. In a large bowl, mix potatoes with
   melted butter and cheese.
3. Mix sour cream and soup together
   and stir into potatoes.
4. Add onions, salt and pepper.
   Mix thoroughly.
5. Put mixture into a greased 9x13-inch
   glass baking dish. Cover with crushed
   potato chips.
6. Bake 45 to 60 minutes.

Serve hot.

Irish Soda Bread

Makes a 9x5-inch loaf

Sensational when served with afternoon tea.

¾ cup sugar
½ cup (1 stick) butter, softened
1 egg
3 cups flour
¼ teaspoon baking soda
1 tablespoon baking powder
¼ teaspoon salt
1¼ cups buttermilk
1 cup raisins
1 teaspoon caraway seed

1. Preheat oven to 350°. Grease and flour
   a 9x5-inch loaf pan. Set aside.
2. Cream together sugar and butter.
   Add egg until well-blended.
3. Sift flour, baking soda, baking powder
   and salt into creamed mixture. Mix well.
4. Stir in buttermilk until blended.
5. Stir in raisins and caraway seed.
6. Spread evenly in loaf pan. Cut a bold
   cross on top of bread. (Prevents cracking
   — ed's. note.) Bake 1 hour until lightly
   browned.
7. Cool in pan 5 minutes. Remove bread
   to wire rack and continue to cool.

**For a round loaf, bread can be baked in a
1½-quart casserole. Cut into wedges to serve.**

Lemon Bubbles

This excellent bread will send you floating.

5 to 6 cups flour
½ cup sugar
1 teaspoon salt
2 packages yeast
1 cup milk
½ cup water
¼ cup (½ stick) butter
2 eggs

Lemon mixture:

½ cup sugar
2 lemon rinds, grated
¼ teaspoon mace
2 tablespoons butter, melted

Begin preparations early in day or 4 hours before serving.

1. In large mixing bowl, combine 2 cups flour, ½ cup sugar, salt and yeast.

2. In medium saucepan over low heat, heat milk, ½ cup water and ¼ cup butter until very warm (120° to 130°).

3. With mixer at low speed, gradually pour liquid into dry ingredients; beat until just mixed.

4. Increase speed to medium, add eggs and beat 2 minutes, occasionally scraping bowl with a rubber spatula.

5. Beat in ½ cup flour, or enough to thicken batter and beat 2 more minutes.

6. With spoon, stir in enough flour (about 2 cups) to make a soft dough.

7. Turn dough onto lightly floured surface and knead until smooth and elastic, about 10 minutes.

8. Shape into ball and place into greased bowl, turning over so top of dough is greased. Cover with towel and let rise in warm place (80° to 85°) until doubled, about 1 hour.

9. Punch down dough. then turn it onto a lightly floured surface and cut in half. Cover with bowl and let stand 15 minutes.

10. In small bowl combine ½ cup sugar, lemon rind and mace. Set aside. Melt 2 tablespoons butter in small saucepan and set aside. Grease a 10-inch angelfood pan.

11. Cut each dough half into 16 pieces. Shape each into a ball by tucking ends under.

12. Place half of balls in angelfood pan, brush with half of melted butter and sprinkle with half of lemon mixture. Repeat with remaining balls, butter and lemon mixture.

13. Cover with towel; let rise until doubled, about 45 minutes.
14. Preheat oven to 350°. Bake 35 minutes or until loaf is golden and sounds hollow when tapped.
15. Cool rolls in pan 5 minutes; remove and cool on wire rack.

Caramel Custard   Serves 8 to 10

a.k.a. Caramelized Custard, Créme Caramel and Flan.

Caramel:
1 cup sugar
2 tablespoons water

Custard:
1 8-ounce package cream cheese
½ cup sugar
5 eggs
2 cups milk
½ teaspoon salt
½ teaspoon vanilla
½ teaspoon lemon rind

This recipe can also be made in individual serving custard cups.
Traditional dessert when serving Paella.

Caramel preparation:
1. Preheat oven to 350°.
2. In saucepan, on medium high heat, melt together sugar and water, stirring constantly until sugar turns an amber color.
3. Pour into 2-quart casserole, whirling mixture to cover bottom and sides. (Sugar will harden quickly.)
4. Let sit while preparing custard.

Custard preparation:
1. In a medium bowl, cream together cream cheese and sugar.
2. Add eggs and beat well.
3. In a small bowl, mix milk with salt, vanilla and lemon rind. Add to cream cheese mixture. Mix thoroughly.
4. Pour liquid into caramel lined casserole.
5. Place casserole in large pan that has been filled with 2-inches of hot water.
6. Bake 45 to 50 minutes until set and golden brown.
7. Remove custard from water and let cool completely before refrigerating.
8. When ready to serve, invert on serving plate.
9. Cut into wedges or spoon into bowls or cups, being sure to spoon caramel sauce over each serving.

Rhubarb Custard Pie

Serves 8 to 10

Even those wary of rhubarb will love this pie.

5 cups rhubarb
3 eggs, slightly beaten
1½ cups sugar
¼ cup flour
¼ teaspoon nutmeg
2 tablespoons butter
prepared pastry dough for 2 9-inch crusts

1. Preheat oven to 350°.
2. Cut rhubarb into 1-inch pieces. Set aside.
3. In a large bowl beat eggs until light.
4. Add sugar, flour and nutmeg. Beat well.
5. Stir rhubarb into egg mixture.
6. Line the bottom of a 9-inch pie plate with pastry dough.
7. Pour filling over unbaked dough. Dot with butter.
8. Cover with pastry. Crimp edges to seal.
9. Make several slits in top pastry.
10. Bake 45 to 50 minutes until crust is golden.
11. Cool on wire rack.

Serve warm or cold.

Key Lime Pie

Serves 8 to 10

Think cool breezes and swaying palm trees.

1 14-ounce can sweetened condensed milk
¼ cup Key lime juice
2 teaspoons Key lime rind, grated
1 egg plus 3 eggs separated
4 teaspoons sugar
1 9-inch prepared pie crust, partially baked OR 1 9-inch graham cracker crust

1. Preheat oven to 350°.
2. In a large bowl beat together condensed milk, Key lime juice and grated lime rind.
3. Add whole egg plus 3 egg yolks. Blend well.
4. Pour into crust.
5. In a separate bowl beat egg whites until stiff (but not dry), gradually adding sugar and beating constantly.
6. Swirl meringue over filling.
7. Bake for 20 minutes.
8. Chill several hours before serving.

Pie In The Sky

Serves 8 to 10

A wonderful, uplifting dessert for lemon lovers.

¼ cup (½ stick) butter
1 8.8-ounce box digestive wheat biscuits, crushed
1 4-ounce package lemon jello
¾ cup boiling water
2 lemons
½ pound (1⅛ cups) superfine sugar
1 8-ounce package cream cheese
¾ cup evaporated milk, chilled

1. In a small saucepan melt butter and mix with crushed biscuits.
2. Line bottom and sides of a 9-inch spring-form pan or a scallop-edged quiche pan with crushed biscuit mixture.
3. Dissolve the jello in the boiling water. Squeeze the lemons into dissolved jello.
4. In a large bowl cream the sugar and cream cheese until light. Beat in jello and lemon juice mixture.
5. In a separate bowl whip cold evaporated milk and fold into cheese mixture.
6. Pour this into the biscuit lined pan and refrigerate for several hours before serving.

Rainbow Punch

Makes 25 8-ounce servings

You'll think you've found a pot of gold.

1 quart orange juice for ice cubes
2 quarts orange juice for punch
2 quarts cranberry juice
2 quarts lemon-lime soda
orange slices for garnish

Requires some advance preparation.

1. The day before serving, place 1 quart of orange juice in several ice cube trays and freeze.
2. Next day, mix together orange juice, cranberry juice and lemon-lime soda in pitcher. Pour over iced orange juice cubes placed in glasses.
3. Garnish with orange slices.

FOOD FOR A CROWD

SAMPLE MENU

Cousin Patsy's Deviled Eggs

Uncle Bill's Spiced Shrimp

Aunt Mim's Ham Loaf

Aunt Vi's Vidalia Onion Pie

Uncle Fred's Pea Salad

Grandma Gert's Super Size Sunday Salad

Aunt Marian's Dinner Rolls

Block Party Brownies

Crowd Size Carrot Cake

Rosy Red Reunion Punch

Grandma is rattling off her pie crust recipe, the cousins are fighting for a chance to crank the handle on the ice cream maker, Uncle Fred is coming back for another helping. Is this a nostalgic memory of holidays past? No! It's just the annual family reunion, or in our more transient neighborhoods, the block party. Try our crowd-sized recipes, and you'll ALL come back for seconds.

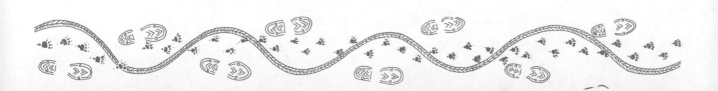

Spinach Dip

Makes I quart

assorted vegetables for dipping
I package frozen spinach,
  thawed, drained and chopped
I package dried vegetable soup mix
I cup mayonnaise
I cup sour cream
I cup water chestnuts, drained and chopped

1. Cut up vegetables, e.g. yellow squash, zucchini squash, sweet potatoes, celery, cauliflower, carrots, broccoli, red or green peppers, cucumber, cherry tomatoes, etc.
2. Combine in a bowl, spinach, soup mix, mayonnaise, sour cream and water chestnuts. Mix well.
3. On a large platter arrange fresh cut up vegetables.
4. Place spinach dip in small glass bowl in center of platter.

Serve cold.

Tortilla Rolls

Makes 60 pieces

Your guests will shout, *Olé!*

I cup cream cheese
I cup sour cream
I cup cheddar cheese, grated
½ cup scallions, chopped
¼ cup green chilies, chopped
¼ cup black olives, chopped
6 10-inch flour tortillas
salsa

1. In a medium bowl, cream together the cream cheese, sour cream and cheddar cheese.
2. Blend in scallions, chilies and olives.
3. Spread evenly over the 6 tortillas.
4. Roll tortillas tightly, place on pan, seam side down, and refrigerate several hours.
5. When ready to serve, slice into I-inch pieces and serve with salsa (see index).

Sausage Cheese Balls

Makes 60 to 65 balls

I pound bulk pork sausage
I pound sharp cheddar cheese
3 cups Bisquick

1. Preheat oven to 350°.
2. Grate cheese.
3. Mix all ingredients together and roll into I-inch balls.
4. Bake for 20 minutes.

Serve hot.

Piquant Cocktail Meatballs

Makes 60

The sauce makes the dish.

2 pounds ground beef
1 cup packaged cornflake crumbs
⅓ cup dried parsley flakes
2 eggs
2 tablespoons soy sauce
¼ teaspoon pepper
½ teaspoon garlic powder
⅓ cup ketchup
2 tablespoons instant
  minced onions (optional)
Cranberry Sauce

Cranberry Sauce:
1 can jellied cranberry sauce
1 12-ounce bottle chili sauce
1 tablespoon lemon juice

1. Preheat oven to 350°.
2. In a large bowl, combine ground beef, cornflake crumbs, parsley flakes, eggs, soy sauce, pepper, garlic powder, ketchup and minced onions. Blend well.
3. Form into small balls and place in large baking dish.
4. Pour Cranberry Sauce (see below) over meatballs.
5. Bake uncovered for 30 to 45 minutes.

Cranberry Sauce preparation:

1. In a medium size pan combine all ingredients and cook over moderate heat, stirring occasionally until mixture is smooth and cranberry sauce is melted.

Cousin Patsy's Deviled Eggs

Makes 24

12 small eggs, hard-boiled
1 8-ounce can deviled ham
3 tablespoons mayonnaise
1 tablespoon Dijon mustard
⅓ cup celery, finely chopped

1. Shell eggs and cut in half WIDTH-wise.
2. Separate yolks and place them in a medium bowl. Refrigerate whites.
3. To the yolks, add ham, mayonnaise, mustard and celery. Mash thoroughly and fill the egg whites with yolk mixture.

Uncle Bill's Spiced Shrimp

Serves 6 to 8

2 pounds medium shrimp,
  cleaned and cooked
1 red onion, thinly sliced
1 lemon, thinly sliced
2 bay leaves
¾ cup salad oil
¾ cup olive oil
2 cups cider vinegar
½ cup pickling spices
1½ tablespoons crushed peppercorns
1 tablespoon sugar
¼ teaspoon mace
1 2-inch piece of fresh ginger, peeled
½ tablespoon dry mustard

1. Place shrimp, onion, lemon, bay leaves
   and oils in a large jar with a clamp-type
   lid; set aside.
2. In a large saucepan place vinegar,
   pickling spices, peppercorns, sugar, mace,
   ginger and mustard. Bring to a boil for
   1 minute. Cool.
3. Strain liquid into the jar. Cover and
   refrigerate, stirring occasionally.

This will keep for up to 2 weeks.

Gizzy's Cole Slaw

Moist without being watery.

Serves 10 to 12

1 head fresh green cabbage,
  cut into fine noodle-like pieces
5 carrots, shredded
1 large green pepper, shredded
1 large onion, shredded
6 tablespoons white vinegar
3 to 4 tablespoons mayonnaise
1 tablespoon vegetable oil
1 tablespoon black pepper
¼ teaspoon sugar
¼ tablespoon salt
1 8-ounce can crushed pineapple

1. In a large bowl, mix the cabbage pieces
   with carrots, peppers and onions.
2. In a separate bowl blend together
   vinegar, mayonnaise, vegetable oil and
   black pepper. Add salt, sugar and
   pineapple.
3. Pour dressing over the cabbage
   mixture and mix until vegetables
   are completely coated.
4. Chill several hours before serving.

**Gizzy is an 82-year-old widow who once owned a restaurant.
This is her favorite cole slaw recipe.**

Bean Salad

Always a treat!

1 16-ounce can corn
1 16-ounce can wax beans
1 16-ounce can green beans
1 16-ounce can red kidney beans
1 16-ounce can garbanzo beans
1 large green pepper, chopped
1 large red pepper, chopped
3 small onions, thinly sliced,
   separated into rings

Marinade:

1½ cups sugar
⅓ cup corn oil
1⅔ cups vinegar
1 teaspoon salt
1 clove garlic, crushed
½ teaspoon pepper

1. Drain the vegetables well.
2. In a large bowl gently mix all vegetables.
3. In a small saucepan mix all marinade ingredients and heat gently to dissolve the sugar, stirring occasionally.
4. Pour warm marinade over vegetables.
5. Refrigerate overnight or longer. Stir occasionally.
6. To serve, drain, reserving marinade for any leftover salad.

Uncle Fred's Pea Salad

Serves 10 to 12

3 10-ounce packages frozen petite peas
¼ cup dill, dried (¾ cup if fresh), chopped
¼ cup scallions, chopped
¼ cup light mayonnaise
¾ cup sour cream
½ teaspoon salt
¼ teaspoon pepper

1. Blanch the peas in boiling water just to defrost them. Drain in colander.
2. In a medium bowl combine dill, scallions, mayonnaise, sour cream, salt and pepper.
3. Add peas and mix thoroughly.
4. Chill for 24 hours to develop flavor.

49

Doc's Potato Salad

Serves 20

Served at Connecticut State Capitol Luncheons.

Salad:

1 pound bacon
5 pounds potatoes, cooked and peeled
2 cups Bermuda onion, finely chopped
2 cups celery, finely chopped
1 very large green pepper, finely chopped

Dressing:

1½ cups mayonnaise
½ cup French dressing
2 tablespoons barbecue sauce
3 tablespoons bacon drippings
½ cup lemon juice (approximately 3 lemons)

1. Cook bacon, drain on paper toweling, crumble and set aside. (Reserve 3 tablespoons bacon drippings for dressing.)

2. In a large bowl gently mix together potatoes, onions, celery, green pepper and bacon.

3. Mix dressing ingredients together in small bowl. Pour over vegetables and toss gently.

4. Chill in refrigerator overnight for flavors to blend.

Grandma Gert's Super Size Sunday Salad

Serves 10 to 12

Never fails to bring rave reviews.

2 packages chicken-flavored rice mix
8 scallions, thinly sliced
½ green pepper, seeded and diced
½ red pepper, seeded and diced
½ yellow pepper, seeded and diced
¼ cup pimento-stuffed olives, sliced
1 cup celery, diced
1 12-ounce jar artichoke hearts in oil
⅔ cup light mayonnaise
1½ teaspoons curry powder

1. Cook rice as directed, omitting butter and cool in a large bowl.

2. Add scallions, peppers, olives and celery.

3. Drain the artichokes, reserving the oil. Cut them in quarters and add to rice mixture.

4. In a small bowl combine the reserved oil with mayonnaise and curry powder.

5. Mix mayonnaise mixture thoroughly into rice mixture.

6. Refrigerate until ready to serve.

Chicken Cacciatore or "Chicken In The Sauce"   Serves 6 to 8

When Sunday dinner needs to be special.

1 3-pound frying chicken
½ teaspoon paprika
1 medium green pepper
2 medium onions
4 cloves garlic
½ cup oil
1 28-ounce can crushed tomatoes
1 6-ounce can tomato paste
1 teaspoon oregano
1 teaspoon thyme
1 teaspoon basil
1 pound pasta
Parmesan OR Romano cheese

1. Cut chicken into serving-size pieces; sprinkle with paprika and set aside.
2. Dice pepper, onion and garlic.
3. Cover bottom of large stockpot with oil (about $\frac{1}{16}$-inch deep) and begin to sauté diced ingredients until softened.
4. Add chicken and fry all sides until lightly browned.
5. In a blender, place tomatoes, tomato paste, oregano, thyme and basil. Blend at low speed until combined.
6. Pour tomato mixture into saucepan with chicken.
7. Cook initially on medium heat to boiling. Lower heat and simmer. BE CAREFUL not to burn the sauce on the bottom of the pot.
8. Simmer 3½ hours or until chicken is tender. Stir sauce often during cooking.

Serve with cooked spaghetti or macaroni, sprinkled with Parmesan or Romano cheese.

Elegant Chicken

10 whole boneless chicken breasts
4 2½-ounce jars dried beef
20 slices bacon
1 10-ounce can cream of
   mushroom soup, undiluted
2¼ cups sour cream
paprika

**If preparing ahead: Bake for 2½ hours.
Refrigerate, then bake 30 minutes more
before serving.**

Serves 20

1. Preheat oven to 275°.
2. Halve chicken breasts and wrap each
   half first with 2 slices of dried beef, then
   1 piece of bacon. Place in a greased
   8x12-inch baking pan, sides touching.
3. Blend together soup and sour cream
   in medium bowl and pour over
   chicken breasts.
4. Sprinkle with paprika.
5. Refrigerate at this point if desired.
6. Bake uncovered for 3 hours.

Roast Turkey With Stuffing

1 25-pound turkey
1 pound bulk sausage
1 pound ground beef
1 medium onion, chopped
1 clove garlic, crushed
1 cup (2 sticks) butter, melted
2 2-pound bags seasoned stuffing mix
2 cups water

Serves 20

1. Preheat oven to 325°.
2. Prepare turkey for stuffing.
3. In a large bowl mix sausage, beef, onion,
   garlic, butter and stuffing mix.
4. Stuff turkey and place in large baking
   pan. Add 2 cups water to pan. Cover
   with foil.
5. Roast, covered, for 8 hours (20 minutes
   per pound). Baste with liquid in pan every
   2 hours, adding more liquid if needed.

Pasta Pie

Serves 20

3 pounds spaghetti
½ cup (1 stick) butter
8 eggs, beaten
1½ cups Parmesan cheese, grated
   and split into two ¾-cup portions
1 quart spaghetti sauce
3 cups Mozzarella cheese, grated
2 tablespoons basil
1 cup pine nuts, sautéed
   in 2 tablespoons butter
1 cup mushrooms, sliced
½ cup parsley, chopped

1. Preheat oven to 350°.
2. In a large pot cook spaghetti in salted boiling water 5 minutes. Drain and return spaghetti to pot.
3. Toss with butter and set aside to cool. When cool stir in beaten eggs and ¾ cup Parmesan.
4. In a large bowl mix spaghetti sauce, Mozzarella, basil, pine nuts, mushrooms, parsley and remaining ¾ cup Parmesan cheese.
5. Add spaghetti and toss together.
6. Place all mixed ingredients into lasagna pan and bake for 30 minutes until set but not browned.
7. Cut into squares to serve.

Wild West Beans

Serves 10 to 12

Come 'n get it, buckaroos!

½ pound ground beef
10 slices bacon, chopped
½ cup onion, chopped
1 16-ounce can kidney beans, drained
1 16-ounce can large butter beans, drained
1 16-ounce can pork and beans
½ cup brown sugar
⅓ cup white sugar
½ cup ketchup
¼ cup barbecue sauce
2 tablespoons prepared mustard
2 tablespoons molasses
½ teaspoon salt
½ teaspoon pepper
½ teaspoon chili powder

1. Preheat oven to 350°.
2. In a large stockpot, brown beef and bacon. Add onion and cook until tender.
3. Add beans and all seasonings. Mix thoroughly.
4. Pour into large baking dish. Cover and bake for 1 hour.

Aunt Mim's Ham Loaf

Serves 16

2 pounds honey-baked smoked ham
2 pounds lean ground pork
1½ cups dry bread crumbs
4 eggs, well beaten
1½ teaspoons salt
2 cups milk
2 tablespoons parsley, chopped

1. Preheat oven to 350°.
2. Coarsely grind the ham in a food processor.
3. In a large bowl combine the ham, pork, bread crumbs, eggs, salt, milk and parsley. Mix well.
4. Press mixture into 2 loaf pans. Put pans on a tray and bake for 30 minutes.
5. In the meantime prepare Basting Glaze. Mix brown sugar, vinegar and mustard in a saucepan and boil for 1 minute.

Basting Glaze:

½ pound brown sugar
½ cup cider vinegar
1½ tablespoons dry mustard

6. Baste loaves and bake 1 hour longer, basting several times.
7. Remove from oven and chill (or freeze for future use). To serve warm, reheat defrosted loaves for 20 minutes at 325°.
8. Serve sliced with Serving Sauce.

Serving Sauce:

½ cup mayonnaise
½ cup sour cream
¼ cup Dijon mustard
1 tablespoon chives
2 tablespoons horseradish
1 teaspoon lemon juice

Serving Sauce preparation:

1. Combine mayonnaise, sour cream, mustard, chives, horseradish and lemon juice.
2. Cover and refrigerate until ready to serve.

Broccoli Casserole

Serves 10 to 12

1 cup (2 sticks) butter
2 cups cheddar cheese, grated
2 cans cream of mushroom soup
1 cup onions, chopped
2 16-ounce packages frozen chopped broccoli, thawed
1 16-ounce package dry stuffing mix

1. Preheat oven to 350°.
2. In a large stockpot melt butter, adding cheddar cheese and soup; stir until cheese is melted.
3. Add onions and broccoli. Mix well.
4. Stir in stuffing and mix thoroughly.
5. Pour into 2 greased 9-inch cake pans, or 1 oblong 9x13-inch pan.
6. Bake 30 minutes until lightly browned.

Saffron Rice

Serves 8 to 10

¼ cup instant minced onions
¼ cup water
¾ cup (1½ sticks) butter
2 cups rice
pinch of saffron
4 bouillon cubes
4 cups hot water

1. Rehydrate onions in water.
2. Melt butter in saucepan. Add onions, cover with tight-fitting lid and cook over low heat for 5 minutes or until onions are golden.
3. Remove cover and stir in rice.
4. In a small bowl dissolve saffron and bouillon cubes in hot water. Pour over rice.
5. Cover and cook over low heat 30 minutes until rice is done and liquid is absorbed.
6. Fluff rice with fork.

Cheddar Potatoes

Serves 10 to 12

8 large potatoes
1 cup milk
½ cup (1 stick) butter
2 cups cheddar cheese, grated
2 cups sour cream
1 large onion, chopped
1 teaspoon salt
½ teaspoon pepper
1 tablespoon chives
1 teaspoon dill

1. Preheat oven to 350°.
2. In large saucepan, cook potatoes in boiling water 20 minutes, until tender.
3. Drain and cool. Peel skins.
4. In a large bowl, mash potatoes with milk. Set aside.
5. In the top of a double boiler, melt butter. Add cheese and stir until well blended.
6. In a separate bowl mix sour cream with onion and seasonings.
7. Add cheese mixture. Stir well. Add potatoes and mix thoroughly.
8. Place potato mixture in a large greased casserole dish.
9. Bake, uncovered for 45 minutes.
10. Remove from oven and serve hot.

Aunt Vi's Vidalia Onion Pie

Serves 8 to 10

Find out why there's such a fuss about Vidalia onions.

2 pounds Vidalia onions, thinly sliced
½ cup (1 stick) butter
3 eggs, well beaten
1 cup sour cream
¼ teaspoon salt
½ teaspoon pepper
2 to 3 dashes Tabasco sauce
¼ teaspoon nutmeg
1 9-inch pastry shell, unbaked
3 tablespoons Parmesan cheese, freshly grated

1. Preheat oven to 450°.
2. In a large frypan sauté onions in butter.
3. In a large bowl combine eggs, sour cream, salt, pepper, Tabasco and nutmeg.
4. Stir in onions and butter.
5. Pour into pie shell and top with cheese.
6. Bake for 20 minutes.
7. Reduce temperature to 325° and bake for additional 20 minutes or until set.
8. Slice when ready to serve.

May be wrapped in aluminum foil and thick layers of newspaper to keep warm while transporting.

Aunt Marian's Dinner Rolls

Makes 18 rolls

"Outstanding" — easy for the novice — impressive enough for the gourmet.

2 packages dry yeast
2 cups warm water
½ cup oil
¼ cup sugar
2 teaspoons salt
6 cups flour
2 tablespoons butter

1. In a large bowl dissolve yeast in warm water.
2. Add oil, sugar and salt. Mix well.
3. Stir in 5 cups flour until thoroughly mixed.
4. Place dough on board and mix with remaining flour. Knead until smooth and elastic.
5. Place in buttered bowl turning to grease both sides. Cover and let rise 1 hour until doubled in bulk.
6. Punch dough down. Cover and let rise another 45 minutes.
7. Punch dough down again and break off pieces for 18 rolls (the size of a lemon).
8. Place rolls in 2 buttered 9-inch pans (9 rolls each). Cover and let rise 30 minutes.

9. Preheat oven to 375°.

10. Bake 25 to 30 minutes.

11. Remove from oven and immediately rub tops with butter. Let cool in pan 5 minutes, then remove to wire rack to cool.

If you've always been fearful of baking a yeast bread, you've got to make these rolls! Don't be intimidated by three rises; the ingredients are simple and basic, easy to prepare and the results are marvelous! When you see and taste the finished product, it will give you the confidence to continue baking with yeast. "Roll" up your sleeves and go for it!

Block Party Brownies

Makes 2 dozen 2-inch squares

For those who prefer brownies without nuts.

1 cup (2 sticks) butter
6 squares unsweetened chocolate
6 eggs
1 teaspoon salt
3 cups sugar
1½ teaspoons vanilla
1½ cups flour

1. Preheat oven to 300°.

2. Melt butter and chocolate in top of double boiler. Set aside to cool.

3. In large bowl beat together eggs and salt.

4. Slowly beat in sugar.

5. Add chocolate/butter mixture, vanilla and flour. Mix thoroughly.

6. Pour into buttered 9x13-inch pan.

7. Bake for 45 to 50 minutes.

8. Cool in pan on wire rack.

Never Fail Chocolate Cake

Serves 8 to 10

1 egg
1½ cups sugar
½ cup cocoa
1½ cups flour
1 teaspoon baking soda
¼ teaspoon salt
1 teaspoon vanilla
½ cup (1 stick) butter, melted
½ cup boiling water
½ cup buttermilk

1. Preheat oven to 350°.
2. Grease and flour an 8-inch square or a 9-inch round pan.
3. In a large bowl mix together all ingredients in order listed. Beat for 2 minutes.
4. Pour into prepared cake pan.
5. Bake 35 minutes or until toothpick inserted in center comes out clean.
6. Cool in pan on wire rack.

Crowd Size Carrot Cake

One way to get the kids to eat carrots.

Makes 2 dozen 2-inch squares

3 cups carrots, shredded
4 eggs
1 cup oil
2 cups sugar
1 teaspoon baking soda
1 teaspoon baking powder
1 teaspoon salt
2 teaspoons cinnamon
2 cups flour

1. Preheat oven to 325°.
2. In food processor, place carrots, eggs, oil, sugar, baking soda, baking powder, salt and cinnamon. Process until smooth.
3. Add flour, one cup at a time, until completely mixed.
4. Pour into greased 9x13-inch pan.
5. Bake for 50 to 60 minutes or until toothpick inserted in center comes out clean.
6. Cool cake in pan on wire rack.
7. Frost cooled cake with Cream Cheese Frosting.

Cream Cheese Frosting:
¼ cup (½ stick) butter
6 ounces cream cheese
2 teaspoons vanilla
2 cups confectioner's sugar

Cream Cheese Frosting preparation:

1. In a medium bowl, cream together butter and cream cheese.
2. Add vanilla and confectioner's sugar; mix well.

Travel with cake in pan. Slice and serve at destination.

Crème de Menthe Brownies

Makes 2 to 3 dozen

Very attractive when cut into small squares, more like candy.

First layer:
½ cup (1 stick) butter, softened
1 cup sugar
1 teaspoon vanilla
4 eggs
1 16-ounce can chocolate syrup
1 cup flour

Second layer:
½ cup (1 stick) butter, softened
2 cups powdered sugar
2 tablespoons Crème de Menthe

Third layer:
1 cup semi-sweet chocolate chips
6 tablespoons butter

1. Preheat oven to 350°.
2. Combine in a bowl, butter, sugar, vanilla, eggs and chocolate syrup.
3. Add flour slowly and mix.
4. Place in a 9x13-inch ungreased pan.
5. Bake for 27 minutes. Remove and cool.
6. Combine butter, sugar and Crème de Menthe. Spread second layer on cooked and cooled first layer.
7. Melt chocolate chips in microwave with butter. Drizzle third layer on second layer.
8. Refrigerate. Cut into small pieces.

Very rich.

English Dressing

Makes stuffing for 1 20-pound turkey

¾ of a loaf of bread
6 slices bacon, diced
turkey liver, heart and gizzard, chopped
1 cup celery, chopped
1 medium onion, chopped
¼ cup fresh parsley, chopped
salt, pepper, sage and thyme to taste
   OR 1 tablespoon poultry seasoning
1 egg, beaten well

1. Grate bread into crumbs and toast in frypan until browned. Set aside.
2. Fry bacon in frypan until crisp.
3. Add liver, heart and gizzard. Fry 1 minute.
4. Add celery and onion. Sauté 5 minutes.
5. Add parsley and seasonings. Simmer 1 minute.
6. Combine cooked ingredients with bread crumbs. Mix thoroughly.
7. Add egg and mix well.
8. Loosely stuff turkey cavity.

Rosy Red Reunion Punch

Makes 20 8-ounce servings

4 12-ounce cans lemonade concentrate
8 cups cranberry juice
2 quarts blush wine

1. Mix lemonade, cranberry juice and wine.
2. Add to thermal cooler or punch bowl.

When adding to punch bowl make an ice ring with additional cranberry juice. Place this in the bottom of a punch bowl before adding liquids.

AT THE SEASHORE

SAMPLE MENU

Jezebel Jelly Fish

Cool Cucumber Soup

Surf Sandwich

Sand Pail Surprise

Seaside Punch

Kid's Beach Party

Those fortunate enough to reside near the shore are able to frequent the lovely beaches, and a picnic at the shore is particularly enjoyable since appetites are whetted by frolicking in the frothy surf and breathing the sea air. Our recipes will keep you cool under the smiling sun, and they will provide the energy you'll need for that refreshing swim or long stroll to gather seashells.

Kid's Beach Party

Serves 4 to 6

Main Dish Dip:

1 pint of sour cream
1 package dry vegetable soup mix

1. Mix sour cream and soup mix.
2. Cover and refrigerate overnight.

Use one dollop of dip per child in their own container. Margarine tubs work well. Pack extra tubs to replace the ones that fall in the sand.

Main Dish Dippers:

pita bread, cut in wedges
cheese, cut in wedges
vegetables, washed and cut into bite size pieces

Dessert Dip:

1 pint flavored yogurt

Dessert Dippers:

pound cake, cut into hearty strips
fruit, washed and cut into dipping size

Bring lots of fruit juice creating special combinations such as orange/cranberry. Wash cloths make good beach napkins, since they don't easily blow away.

Jezebel Jelly Fish

Serves 6 to 8

Jezebel sauce over cream cheese.

18 ounces pineapple preserves
18 ounces apple jelly
3 ounces horseradish, drained
1 1½-ounce can dry mustard
1 tablespoon cracked pepper
2 8-ounce packages cream cheese

1. In a medium bowl beat together preserves, jelly, horseradish, mustard and pepper. Refrigerate for several days to allow flavors to meld.
2. Press cream cheese into a greased FISH-SHAPED mold. Chill.
3. To serve, unmold cream cheese "fish" onto serving dish. Pour sauce over "fish." Spread this on your favorite crackers.
4. Extra sauce can be stored in small jars.

Gold Rush Coleslaw

Makes 3 quarts

There's coleslaw, and then there's coleslaw. They'll rush for more!.

2½ pounds cabbage, shredded
1 large clove garlic, crushed
8 ounces sour cream
2 tablespoons sugar
2 tablespoons white vinegar
1 teaspoon curry
¼ teaspoon salt
¼ teaspoon pepper
¼ cup walnuts, chopped
½ cup golden raisins

1. Place shredded cabbage in a large bowl.
2. In a separate bowl mix together garlic, sour cream, sugar, vinegar, curry, salt and pepper.
3. Pour over cabbage and toss.
4. Add nuts and raisins. Mix thoroughly.
5. Let coleslaw stand at room temperature for 30 minutes to marinate.
6. After marinating toss and serve immediately or refrigerate until serving time.

Pam's Veggie Salad

Serves 6 to 8

No cooking involved here.

2 10-ounce packages frozen mixed vegetables, thawed
2 cucumbers, diced
12 radishes, diced
6 scallions, sliced
1 cup celery, diced

Dressing:

½ cup mayonnaise
1 teaspoon salt
¼ teaspoon pepper
1 teaspoon garlic powder
1 tablespoon lemon juice

1. Combine mixed vegetables, cucumbers, radishes, scallions and celery in a large bowl.
2. When ready to serve, pour dressing on salad and toss to coat evenly.

Dressing preparation:

1. Prepare dressing by blending together the mayonnaise, salt, pepper, garlic powder and lemon juice. Chill several hours in the refrigerator before adding to vegetables.

63

Chicken Aloha Salad

Serves 4 to 6

4 cups cooked chicken, diced
1 cup celery, chopped
1 cup seedless red grapes, halved
½ cup crushed pineapple (reserve liquid)
⅔ cup mayonnaise
3 tablespoons reserved pineapple syrup
¼ tablespoon pepper

1. In a large bowl, combine chicken with celery, grapes and pineapple.

2. In a small bowl, mix mayonnaise with reserved pineapple syrup and pepper. Pour over salad ingredients and toss gently.

3. Cover and refrigerate until ready to serve.

San Francisco Chioppino

Serves 10 to 12

1 large yellow onion, finely chopped
4 small red peppers, finely chopped
¾ cup olive oil
¼ cup fresh marjoram, chopped
2 tablespoons fresh rosemary, chopped
2 tablespoons fresh sage, chopped
2 tablespoons fresh thyme, chopped
¼ cup fresh basil, chopped
½ cup fresh parsley, chopped
   **(If fresh herbs are unavailable,
   use one-quarter as much dried.)**
4 cloves garlic, crushed
40 raw cockle clams
2 large cooked crabs, cleaned and cracked
   OR cooked lobster as a substitute
36 raw prawns
2 pounds sea bass, rock fish, striped bass,
   or other firm fish
3 28-ounce cans solid packed tomatoes
2 tablespoons salt
2 teaspoons pepper
1 cup dry white wine

1. In a large frypan sauté onions and peppers in olive oil until golden. Add herbs and garlic and set aside.

2. Arrange clams in bottom of large stockpot. Layer crab, then prawns, then sea bass on top.

3. Mix together tomatoes, salt and pepper in separate bowl. Add to stockpot along with cooked vegetables, herbs and garlic. Bring to a boil, lower heat and simmer 30 minutes.

4. Add wine. Simmer another 10 minutes.

Cool Cucumber Soup

Serves 4 to 6

4 large cucumbers
4 scallions (white part only), sliced
2 tablespoons butter
1 teaspoon oil
2 tablespoons flour
2½ cups chicken broth
½ cup milk
1½ tablespoons lemon juice
2 teaspoons dill
½ teaspoon salt
¼ teaspoon pepper
2 cups sour cream
½ cup fresh mint leaves

1. Peel, seed and slice cucumbers.
2. In large frypan sauté cucumbers and scallions in butter and oil for 10 minutes.
3. Stir in flour and cook for 1 minute. Stir frequently.
4. Heat broth and milk. Stir into cucumbers.
5. Add lemon juice, dill, salt and pepper. Simmer gently for 10 minutes until thick. Set aside to cool.
6. Purée in food processor until smooth.
7. Place soup in bowl, stir in sour cream and refrigerate overnight.

Garnish with mint before serving.

Famous Fish Chowder

Serves 6 to 8

2 pounds haddock, cut in serving pieces
3 medium onions, chopped
4 potatoes, cubed
¼ cup celery with leaves, chopped
1 bay leaf
2½ teaspoons salt
¼ teaspoon cayenne pepper
½ teaspoon chili powder
½ cup (1 stick) butter
¼ teaspoon dill
¼ teaspoon white pepper
2 cups boiling water
2 cups light cream
¼ cup parsley, chopped
1 cup corn (optional)

1. Preheat oven to 375°.
2. Place all ingredients except cream in 3-quart casserole. Cover.
3. Bake for 1 hour.
4. Heat cream in saucepan to boiling point. Add to chowder.
5. Garnish with chopped parsley.

Add 1 cup corn if desired.
Serve with salad and French bread.

Surf Sandwich

Serves 6

Two hands are needed to eat this hearty sandwich.

12 slices bacon
12 slices egg bread
mayonnaise to taste
2 cups lettuce
2 cups tomato, sliced
1 pound lobster meat, cooked and sliced

1. Cook bacon until crisp. Drain on paper towels and set aside.
2. Spread bread with mayonnaise.
3. Layer greens, tomato, bacon and lobster on 6 slices of bread. Cover with remaining 6 slices.
4. To serve cut sandwiches in half.

Bluefish With Meringue

Serves 2 to 4

1 bluefish fillet from a large fish
  OR 2 fillets from smaller fish
1 small onion, sliced
1 fresh tomato, skinned and sliced
1 teaspoon parsley, chopped
¼ teaspoon thyme, dried or
  1 teaspoon fresh
½ teaspoon salt
¼ teaspoon pepper
1 cup Cream Sauce (see below)
3 egg whites
¼ cup Parmesan cheese, grated

1. Place fish in shallow baking dish.
2. Broil for 10 minutes.
3. Remove from broiler. Preheat oven to 350°.
4. Arrange slices of onion and tomatoes on top of bluefish. Season with parsley, thyme, salt and pepper.
5. Pour Cream Sauce over fish and vegetables.
6. In a small bowl whip egg whites until stiff. Spread over fish and sprinkle with cheese.
7. Bake at 350° for 20 minutes or until meringue has browned.

Cream Sauce:

2 tablespoons butter
2 tablespoons flour
1 cup milk
¼ teaspoon salt
⅛ teaspoon pepper

Cream Sauce preparation: (makes one cup)

1. Over low heat melt butter in saucepan.
2. Add flour and whisk until smooth.
3. Slowly add milk, salt and pepper and continue to stir with whisk.
4. Cook, stirring until thickened and smooth.

Picnic Pie

Serves 6 to 8

1 package pie crust mix
1 pound mild Italian or turkey sausage
1 tablespoon oil
1 cup onion, chopped
2 packages frozen chopped spinach,
   thawed and well drained
¾ teaspoon oregano
½ teaspoon fennel seed, crushed
2 eggs, lightly beaten
⅛ teaspoon salt
⅛ teaspoon pepper
1 cup Ricotta cheese
¼ cup milk

1. Preheat oven to 375°.
2. Prepare pie crust mix according to package directions. Wrap and chill 1 hour.
3. In a large pot over medium heat, brown sausage in oil. Remove from pan with slotted spoon, crumble and set aside.
4. Cook onions in same pot until softened.
5. Stir in spinach, oregano and fennel. Cook 5 minutes until liquid is evaporated.
6. Remove from heat and add eggs, salt and pepper. Mix thoroughly.
7. In a separate bowl mix cheese and milk.
8. Roll out three-quarters of pie dough and line a greased springform pan.
9. Layer half the spinach mixture, half the sausage, all of the cheese mixture. Add the remaining sausage then spinach mixture last.
10. Roll out remaining pie dough and cover filling. Crimp and seal dough.
11. Bake 1 hour until golden. Cool.
12. Unmold, wrap and refrigerate.
13. Cut into wedges and wrap each piece separately for a picnic.

Serve with a tossed salad.

Chicken With Artichokes

Serves 4 to 6

Lightly aromatic.

2 jars marinated artichoke hearts,
  drained, liquid reserved
1 tablespoon olive oil
3 chicken breasts, split, skinned
  and boned
1 clove garlic, crushed
1¼ teaspoons salt
½ teaspoon basil
½ teaspoon oregano
½ teaspoon pepper
1 tablespoon parsley, chopped
½ pound mushrooms, halved
½ cup sherry

1. Preheat oven to 350°.
2. Mix reserved artichoke liquid with oil
  in heavy frypan and heat.
3. Brown chicken on all sides and remove
  to casserole dish.
4. Mix garlic, salt, basil, oregano, pepper,
  parsley and mushrooms with remaining
  sauce in skillet.
5. Pour over chicken.
6. Cover and bake 1 hour.
7. Uncover and add sherry and artichokes.
8. Bake 10 minutes longer.

Serve hot over rice or noodles.

Sand Pail Surprise

Serves 12

Young and not-so-young will get a kick out of this dessert.

1 20-ounce package vanilla sandwich cookies
1 cup confectioner's sugar
½ cup (1 stick) butter
2 8-ounce packages cream cheese
2 5½-ounce packages instant vanilla pudding
3½ cups milk
1 12-ounce container Cool Whip
seashell candies
gummy fish

1. Finely crush cookies in food processor.
  Set aside.
2. In a large bowl, cream together confectioner's sugar, butter and cream cheese.
3. Add pudding and milk. Mix until creamy.
4. Fold in Cool Whip.
5. Beginning and ending with crushed
  cookies, alternate crumbs and pudding
  mix in a large CLEAN sand pail.
6. Sprinkle top with seashell candies
  or gummy fish.
7. Serve with a CLEAN shovel.

To make "Dirt" instead of "Sand", substitute *chocolate* sandwich cookies and place all ingredients in a clay flower pot. Sprinkle top with gummy worms and serve with a garden spade.

Great Grandmother's Marble Cake   Serves 12

From Baden, Germany to America.

1 cup butter
2 cups sugar
4 eggs, separated
1 teaspoon vanilla
4 cups flour
2 teaspoons baking powder
1 cup milk
3 tablespoons cocoa
¼ teaspoon cinnamon
confectioner's sugar

1. Preheat oven to 375°.
2. In a large bowl cream together butter and sugar. Beat until fluffy.
3. Beat in egg yolks one at a time.
4. Add vanilla and beat well.
5. Add flour and baking powder alternating with milk. Blend until light and airy.
6. Put half the mixture in another bowl and gradually blend in cocoa and cinnamon until smooth.
7. In a separate bowl, beat egg whites until soft peaks form.
8. Slowly blend half the beaten egg whites into the chocolate mixture and one half into the vanilla mixture.
9. Spoon chocolate and vanilla mixture alternately into greased and bread-crumbed springform pan.
10. Bake for one hour until toothpick inserted in center comes out clean.
11. Cool in pan on wire rack.
12. Dust with confectioner's sugar before cake cools. DO NOT remove sides until cake has cooled.

Great Take Along Cake

Easy to prepare, mixed by hand.

Makes 2 dozen pieces

2 cups flour
2 cups sugar
¾ cup (1½ sticks) butter
1 cup water
4 tablespoons cocoa
2 eggs
½ cup buttermilk
1 teaspoon baking soda
1 teaspoon vanilla
1 teaspoon cinnamon

1. Preheat oven to 400°.
2. Grease 10½x15½-inch jellyroll pan.
3. In a large bowl mix flour and sugar together. Set aside.
4. In a small saucepan heat butter, water and cocoa until they come to a rapid boil.
5. Pour immediately into the flour and sugar mixture and beat vigorously until well blended.
6. Stir in unbeaten eggs, buttermilk, baking soda, vanilla and cinnamon. Mix thoroughly.
7. Pour into prepared jellyroll pan.
8. Bake for 20 minutes.
9. Ice immediately when removed from oven.
10. Cool in pan on wire rack.

Icing:

½ cup (1 stick) butter
4 tablespoons cocoa
1 pound box confectioner's sugar
4 to 6 tablespoons milk
1 teaspoon vanilla

Icing preparation:

1. In a large saucepan melt butter.
2. Stir in cocoa, confectioner's sugar, milk and vanilla. Mix thoroughly.
3. Spread over warm cake.

Last Dip Of Summer

When was the last time you had fun with fondue?

Makes 1 quart

4 cups brown sugar
1¼ cups milk
½ cup (1 stick) butter
½ cup semi-sweet chocolate
¼ cup Cointreau or Créme de Cacao
¼ cup cognac

Leftover bits of cake, cookies or marshmallows can be used as "dippers."

1. Combine sugar, milk, butter and chocolate in a saucepan.
2. Stir over low heat until sugar is dissolved and butter is melted.
3. Add Cointreau or Créme de Cacao and cognac.
4. Pour into a fondue pot and serve with assorted fruits and cakes.

Granny's Watermelon Pickle

Makes 5 cups of pickle

Once you've tasted these pickles, you'll want them over and over again.

2 pounds watermelon rind, skinned and chunked (leave a little pink)
2 quarts water
¼ cup salt
2 cups sugar
I pint vinegar
I lemon, thinly sliced
I tablespoon cinnamon
I teaspoon whole cloves
I teaspoon allspice

1. Soak trimmed watermelon rind overnight in I quart water plus ¼ cup salt. Drain.
2. Place soaked rinds in large stockpot. Add I quart water to cover.
3. Bring water to boil and cook rind 30 minutes, until tender. Drain.
4. Combine sugar, vinegar, lemon, cinnamon, cloves and allspice to make pickling fluid. Add to stockpot with rind and boil until transparent. (15 to 20 minutes.) Cool slightly.
5. Place pickles with liquid in boiled jars. Seal and refrigerate at least I week before serving.

Homemade pickles make wonderful Christmas gifts.

Seaside Punch

Makes 12 8-ounce servings

Refreshingly non-alcoholic.

1½ cups sugar
1½ cups water
3 cups grapefruit juice
3 cups orange juice
¾ cup lime juice
I quart ginger ale

1. In a large saucepan, combine sugar and water. Stir until dissolved. Bring to a boil. Let boil 5 minutes without stirring. Chill.
2. Add juices and ginger ale and pour over ice.

You may mix sugar, water, grapefruit, orange juice and lime juice ahead of time. Add ginger ale when you reach your destination.

CONCERT DINING

SAMPLE MENU

White Wine

Conductor's Caviar

Symphony Salad

Light Melody Mold

Keyboard Bread

Sonata Squares

A blushing sunset accompanies the sweet strains of music at a summer concert. Brass instruments gleam in the dusky twilight, and the tinkling of champagne glasses harmonizes perfectly. Select the appropriate fare and you will be guaranteed a sensory bouquet. Simple or elaborate, you are the maestro, free to conduct the evening as you choose. Our recipes will assure a standing ovation and repeated shouts of *Bravo.*

Conductor's Caviar

Serves 12

A luscious, low calorie combination perfect for concerts.

6 tablespoons butter
2 small onions, chopped
4 cloves fresh garlic, crushed
2 pounds fresh mushrooms,
   coarsely chopped in food processor
1 tablespoon dry sherry
2 tablespoons capers, drained
2 tablespoons fresh parsley, chopped
4 tablespoons fresh dill, chopped
½ teaspoon black pepper, freshly ground
pumpernickel or rye bread
sour cream

1. Melt the butter in a frypan.
2. Add onions and garlic. Stir for 3 minutes on medium high heat.
3. Reduce heat to medium and add mushrooms. Cook 10 to 12 minutes or until liquid is absorbed.
4. Remove from heat and stir in sherry.
5. Add capers, parsley, dill and black pepper. Mix together and store in a covered bowl.
6. Chill 4 hours or keep in refrigerator until ready to serve.
7. Serve at room temperature on small pumpernickel or rye breads that have been spread with a thin layer of sour cream.

Shrimp Spread

Serves 10 to 12

Couldn't be easier.

1 8-ounce package cream cheese
   and chives, softened
½ cup mayonnaise
2 tablespoons dry onions
1 teaspoon Worcestershire sauce
2 8-ounce cans tiny shrimp
1 loaf of round bread,
   pumpernickel or pumpernickel
   with raisins

1. In a mixing bowl, beat together cream cheese and mayonnaise until smooth. Add dry onions, Worcestershire sauce and mix again. Fold in shrimp. Set aside.
2. Slice round bread in half, horizontally, and scoop out ½-inch of bottom half.
3. Fill bottom half of bread with cheese and shrimp mixture. Put top half on mixture. Chill.
4. When ready to serve slice in wedges.

Smartini

Serves 2 to 4

A cool soup to accompany hot music.

1 can cream of celery soup, undiluted
1 soup can of cracked ice
¼ cup chopped cucumbers
¼ cup sour cream or sour* half-and-half
chopped dill as garnish

* Add 1 teaspoon vinegar to half-and-half

1. Blend all ingredients in food processor.
2. Serve in mugs or cups with spoons. Garnish with dill.

Symphony Salad

Serves 6 to 8

You will be "in tune" when you serve this salad.

2 pounds sirloin steak
½ cup (1 stick) butter
¾ pound mushrooms, sliced
1 9-ounce package frozen artichoke hearts, thawed
1 cup celery, finely chopped
1 pint cherry tomatoes, halved
2 tablespoons chives, chopped
2 tablespoons parsley, chopped
2 cups salad dressing (see below)

Salad Dressing:

1½ cups oil
½ cup wine vinegar
6 shallots, minced
⅓ cup fresh parsley, chopped
⅓ cup fresh dill, chopped
½ teaspoon salt
¼ teaspoon pepper
⅛ teaspoon Tabasco
1 tablespoon Dijon mustard

1. Cut steak into ½- to 1-inch cubes and sauté* in ¼ cup butter until cooked (4 to 5 minutes).
2. Place in large salad bowl.
3. Sauté mushrooms in remaining ¼-cup butter and cool; place in bowl with steak.
4. Add artichokes, celery, tomatoes, chives and parsley.
5. Toss with salad dressing. Cover and marinate overnight.
6. Remove from refrigerator at least 1 hour before serving.

* Sirloin can be sautéed, oven-broiled or charcoal broiled.
Best served at room temperature.

Salad Dressing preparation: (for 2 cups)
Whisk all ingredients together and pour over salad.

Recipe must be made ahead.

Curry Pasta Salad

Serves 8

Great for those not wishing to turn into tubby tubas.

1 pound medium pasta shells
  cooked al dente
2 medium apples, peeled, cored and diced
1 teaspoon lemon juice
1 sweet red pepper, cut into small strips
3 celery stalks, finely chopped
¼ cup walnut pieces
¼ cup raisins

Dressing:

¼ cup light mayonnaise
¼ cup plain yogurt
¼ cup milk
1 teaspoon curry
½ teaspoon salt
¼ teaspoon pepper

1. Run cold water over pasta shells to cool.
2. In a large bowl, toss apple pieces in lemon juice.
3. Combine remaining ingredients with apples.
4. Add cooked pasta and mix well.
5. Pour on dressing, toss and refrigerate several hours before serving.

Dressing preparation:

1. Mix all ingredients together.

Ginger Broccoli Salad

Serves 4

4 dried shiitake mushrooms
1 bunch broccoli
¼ pound fresh mushrooms, sliced
½ cup carrots, diced
3 tablespoons sesame seeds, toasted
¼ cup pickled ginger, with liquid
¼ cup tahini
2 teaspoons tamari

Ingredients can be found in oriental food stores and larger supermarkets.

1. Soak shiitake mushrooms in hot water for 30 minutes. Drain and squeeze dry, then slice.
2. Cut broccoli into florets and steam with shiitakes until tender. Refresh under cold water, drain and transfer to a mixing bowl.
3. Add fresh mushrooms, carrots, sesame seeds and toss.
4. Drain 3 tablespoons of liquid from the ginger container into a small bowl.
5. Mince ginger and add to bowl with tahini and tamari. Mix well.
6. Pour over vegetables and toss.

Refrigerate until ready to serve.

Light Melody Mold

Serves 10 to 12

Con allegro.

2 1-pound cans apricot halves,
  drained, syrup reserved
1 6-ounce package orange jello
⅛ teaspoon salt
1 6-ounce can orange juice concentrate
2 tablespoons lemon juice
7 ounces of ginger ale or lemon-lime soda
fresh or canned apricot halves
  for garnish

1. Drain apricots and reserve 1½ cups syrup.
2. Purée apricots in blender (about 2 cups).
3. In saucepan combine reserved syrup, jello and salt. Bring to boil over medium high heat.
4. Remove from heat, add apricots, orange juice concentrate and lemon juice. Stir to blend.
5. Pour into a 6½-cup greased mold.
6. Slowly pour soda into mold. With knife, mix slowly for marble effect.
7. Chill until firm.
8. When ready to serve, unmold on serving platter and surround with fresh or canned apricot halves.

Shirley's Seafood Casserole

Serves 6 to 8

You'll get a standing ovation when you serve this masterpiece.

½ cup (1 stick) butter
1 pound shrimp, cleaned
1 pound crab OR
  ½ pound lobster meat
1 pound sea scallops
½ teaspoon salt
¼ teaspoon pepper
1 clove garlic, crushed
¼ cup flour
1½ cups skim milk
2 tablespoons dry white vermouth
1 cup bread crumbs
¼ cup Parmesan cheese, grated
dash paprika

1. Preheat oven to 350°.
2. Melt ¼ cup butter in frypan. Add seafood and stir. Add salt, pepper and garlic. Cook until seafood is cooked through.
3. Add flour, stirring constantly. Slowly add milk, continuing to stir. Cook until thickened.
4. Add vermouth and transfer to casserole dish.
5. In a small saucepan, melt remaining ¼ cup butter.
6. Add bread crumbs and cook until lightly browned.
7. Add cheese and paprika. Mix well and sprinkle over seafood.
8. Bake for 25 to 30 minutes until browned.

One Hour Paella

Serves 4

A well orchestrated time saver.

4 Italian sausages (about 12 ounces)
  cut into 1-inch pieces
1 medium onion, chopped
1 small red pepper, chopped
1 small green pepper, chopped
2 large cloves garlic, crushed
2 boneless chicken breasts, skinned
  and cut into 1-inch pieces
1½ cups long grain rice
2¼ cups chicken broth
salt and freshly ground pepper to taste
12 medium shrimp with shells
2 medium tomatoes, peeled,
  quartered and seeded
pinch of ground saffron
French bread

1. Sauté sausage in heavy stockpot over medium-high heat until cooked through, 5 to 6 minutes. Reduce heat to medium.
2. Add onion, peppers and garlic. Sauté until onion is soft, about 5 minutes.
3. Add chicken and sauté until lightly browned, 6 to 8 minutes.
4. Add rice and sauté until translucent, 2 to 3 minutes.
5. Add broth, season with salt and pepper.
6. Bring to a boil, reduce heat to low, cover and simmer until almost all liquid is absorbed, 20 to 25 minutes.
7. Stir rice mixture with fork. Add shrimp, tomatoes and saffron. Cover and cook until all liquid is absorbed and prawns are pink, 8 to 10 minutes.

Serve hot with French bread.

Spinach Quiche

Serves 16

2 unbaked 9-inch pastry shells
1 tablespoon butter, softened
1 pound bacon
6 eggs
3 cups half-and-half
¾ teaspoon salt
pinch nutmeg
pinch sugar
pinch cayenne pepper
⅛ teaspoon pepper, freshly ground
2 packages frozen chopped spinach,
  thawed and drained
¼ cup scallions, chopped
¼ cup parsley, chopped
2 cups cheddar cheese, grated
½ cup mushrooms, sliced

1. Preheat oven to 400°.
2. Rub soft butter over surface of pastry shells.
3. Fry bacon until crisp. Drain and crumble.
4. Combine eggs, half-and-half, seasonings, well-drained thawed spinach, scallions and parsley. Mix thoroughly and set aside.
5. Sprinkle crumbled bacon and grated cheese in pastry shells. Top with mushrooms.
6. Pour on cream mixture.
7. Bake 10 to 15 minutes. Reduce to 300° and bake 40 additional minutes.

Crabe Michelle Avec Sauce Louis   Serves 4

Crabe Michelle:

2 eggs
2 cups long grain rice
3 bay leaves
2 tablespoons butter
1 pound fresh crabmeat
2 tablespoons chives for garnish
½ teaspoon paprika for garnish

Sauce Louis:

1 cup mayonnaise
⅓ cup heavy cream
5 tablespoons chili sauce
1½ tablespoons Worcestershire sauce
¼ cup green pepper, chopped
¼ cup Bermuda onion, chopped
2 tablespoons lemon juice
⅓ cup chablis wine

1. Hard boil 2 eggs. Cool and slice.
2. Cook rice according to package directions with bay leaves and butter.
3. Add crabmeat to Sauce (below) and heat until warmed.
4. Place cooked rice in serving platter. Pour crabmeat sauce over rice and garnish with egg, chives and paprika.

Sauce preparation:

1. In a saucepan combine mayonnaise, cream, chili sauce, Worcestershire sauce, green pepper, onion, lemon juice and wine. Heat throroughly 5 to 10 minutes.

Herbed Bubble Bread

Sure to get rave reviews.

⅔ cup Parmesan cheese, grated
1 tablespoon parsley
½ teaspoon basil
½ teaspoon garlic powder
½ teaspoon paprika
3 cups buttermilk baking mix
¾ cup sour cream or non-fat yogurt
¼ cup skim milk
¼ cup (½ stick) butter, melted

Makes 1 dozen "rolls"

1. Preheat oven to 350°.
2. Combine cheese, parsley, basil, garlic powder and paprika in a shallow bowl.
3. In a separate bowl combine baking mix, sour cream and milk to form a soft dough. Knead dough for 1 minute and turn onto a floured surface. Shape into 2-inch balls.
4. Roll balls in melted butter and then in herb mixture.
5. Place side-by-side in greased 8-inch cake pan and bake for 25 minutes.
6. Cool before removing from pan.

Keyboard Bread

Play this without a cutting instrument — simply pull apart.

5 cups flour
3 packages dry yeast
2 tablespoons sugar
1 teaspoon salt
1½ cups milk
⅓ cup butter
1 egg
1 cup (2 sticks) butter, melted

1. In large bowl of mixer stir together 1½ cups flour, yeast, sugar and salt; set aside.
2. In saucepan, heat milk and the ⅓ cup butter until very warm (120° to 130°) and pour over flour-yeast mixture.
3. Add egg and beat 3 minutes at medium speed, scraping bowl occasionally.
4. Add 1 cup flour and beat 3 minutes longer.
5. Stir in remaining 2½ cups flour and mix with wooden spoon until thoroughly blended.
6. Grease top of dough.
7. Cover and let rise in warm place until double in bulk, about 30 minutes.
8. Turn out on lightly floured surface and knead until smooth.
9. Divide dough in half and roll out each half into 18x12-inch rectangle.
10. Cut lengthwise in ¼-inch strips, then crosswise in 3-inch pieces.
11. Dip each piece in melted butter, then toss helter-skelter into a 10-inch angelfood pan.
12. Cover and let rise in warm place until double in bulk, about 1 to 1½ hours.
13. Preheat oven to 425°.
14. Bake on bottom rack about 20 minutes or until golden brown.
15. Remove bread from pan and cool on rack.

Sonata Squares

Dessert for the virtuoso!

Makes 3 dozen 2-inch squares

5 cups flour
1 pound butter
1 cup sugar
1 pound raspberry jam

1. Preheat oven to 375°.
2. Mix first three ingredients (dough will be somewhat crumbly) and press half of dough into a jellyroll pan.
3. Spread raspberry jam over entire surface of dough.
4. Cover with remaining half of dough keeping dough crumbly. Pat down gently.
5. Bake for 25 minutes.
6. Cool on rack in pan.

Island Chess Pie

Serves 8

From Maine via Georgia — this recipe marches to a different drummer.

½ cup butter (1 stick), softened
1½ cups sugar
4 eggs
1 tablespoon vinegar
1 teaspoon vanilla
1 unbaked 9-inch pie crust

1. Preheat oven to 350°.
2. Cream together butter and sugar.
3. Beat in eggs.
4. Add vinegar and vanilla. Beat well.
5. Pour into unbaked pie shell.
6. Bake 50 to 60 minutes until set, golden brown and beginning to crack in the middle.

Serve warm or cold with whipped cream.

Grapes in Sour Cream

Serves 10 to 12

An elegant finale to any picnic.

1 pound seedless green grapes
1 pound seedless red grapes
1 pound seedless white grapes
2 tablespoons orange juice
⅔ cup sour cream
2 tablespoons grated orange rind
brown sugar

1. Remove grapes from stems and place in pretty glass bowl.
2. Combine orange juice, sour cream and grated orange rind.
3. Toss gently with grapes.
4. Sprinkle with brown sugar.

To serve, spoon grapes into clear glasses.

Mom's Texas Pecan Cake

Serves 16

1 pound butter
2 cups sugar
6 eggs, well beaten
1 tablespoon vanilla
4 cups flour
1½ teaspoons baking powder
4 cups pecan halves
2 cups golden raisins

1. Preheat oven to 350°.
2. Grease and flour angelfood pan.
3. Cream butter and sugar until fluffy.
4. Beat in eggs and vanilla.
5. In a separate bowl sift flour and baking powder three times.
6. Add nuts and raisins to flour.
7. Blend flour and butter mixtures together.
8. Pour into tube pan and bake 1½ to 2 hours.
9. Cool 15 minutes before taking cake out of pan.

Peanut Butter And Chocolate Mini Cheesecakes

Makes 12

¾ cup chocolate covered graham crackers, crushed
½ cup semi-sweet chocolate
1½ cups cream cheese, softened
½ cup sugar
1 teaspoon vanilla
½ cup milk
2 eggs
⅓ cup peanut butter

1. Preheat oven to 325°.
2. Line 2½-inch muffin cups with 12 paper muffin cups.
3. Crush graham crackers and place 1 tablespoon in each muffin paper. Set aside.
4. Melt chocolate in double boiler and set aside to cool.
5. In a small bowl beat the cream cheese, sugar and vanilla together until fluffy.
6. Add milk and eggs. Beat until blended. (DO NOT OVERBEAT.)
7. Divide mixture in half.
8. Gradually stir half the cheese mixture into melted chocolate until well blended.
9. Add peanut butter to remaining half of cheese mixture. Stir until blended.
10. Spoon 2 tablespoons of the peanut butter mixture in each muffin cup; spread evenly.

11. Spoon 2 tablespoons of the chocolate mixture over the peanut butter mixture; spread evenly.
12. Bake 20 to 25 minutes until set.
13. Cool cheesecakes on wire rack. Chill to store.
14. To serve, remove papers and invert.

Peach And Raspberry Kuchen

Serves 8 to 10

½ cup (1 stick) unsalted butter
⅓ cup sugar
2 tablespoons light brown sugar
1 large egg
½ teaspoon vanilla
½ teaspoon almond extract
1½ cups flour
1 teaspoon baking powder
¾ teaspoon salt
3 peaches
1 pint raspberries
1 tablespoon sugar for sprinkling
currant jelly, melted

1. Preheat oven to 375°.
2. In a small saucepan, cook butter over moderate heat until golden brown, being careful not to burn. Let cool. Chill just until it is no longer liquid.
3. In a large bowl, cream together the browned butter and sugars.
4. Beat in egg, vanilla and almond extract.
5. Into the bowl, sift the flour, baking powder and salt. Mix dough until combined.
6. Press dough into bottom and sides of 9-inch fluted tart pan with removable bottom.
7. In a saucepan of boiling water, blanch the peaches for 1 minute. Drain and rinse under cold water.
8. Remove skin from peaches; halve and cut into ⅛-inch slices.
9. Arrange slices decoratively in pie shell.
10. Sprinkle peaches with sugar and bake on lower rack of oven for 20 minutes.
11. Remove pan and decoratively arrange raspberries on pie.
12. Return to oven and cook an additional 10 minutes.
13. When done, brush kuchen with melted jelly.
14. Cool in pan on wire rack.

Fireworks Display

SAMPLE MENU

Shrimp Sparklers

Sourdough Bread

Pretzels With Pizzaz

Curry Explosion Chicken

Rockets Julienne

Grand Finale Pie

Who is not enchanted by the magic of a fireworks display? Everyone becomes a child as the sky above explodes with color and light. In this section, we have concentrated on recipes which are particularly portable and easy to prepare, although taste and eye appeal have not been sacrificed. These dazzling dishes can compete with any pyrotechnical display and will add sizzle and sparkle to your evening of awe.

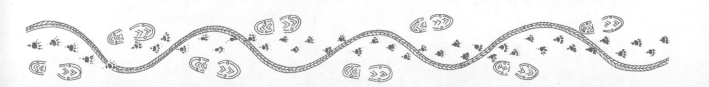

Ham And Cheese Rollups

Makes 24 rollups

8 ounces cream cheese
2 tablespoons horseradish
1 tablespoon chives, chopped
24 slices smoked ham
24 slices Swiss cheese

1. Mix cream cheese, horseradish and chives until smoothly blended.
2. Layer one slice of Swiss cheese on top of one slice of ham.
3. Spread a thin layer of horseradish-cream cheese mixture on the top of the cheese.
4. Roll so that the ham forms the outermost layer. Then pin with a toothpick.

Refrigerate until ready to serve.

Pretzels With Pizzazz

Makes 2 quarts

Flavor improves with age.

12-ounce bottle buttery flavored popcorn oil
1 package dry ranch dressing mix
1½ teaspoons lemon pepper
1½ teaspoons garlic powder
1½ teaspoons dill
1½ teaspoons grated Romano cheese
2 boxes (12½-ounces each), hard sourdough pretzels

1. Preheat oven to 250°.
2. Mix all ingredients except pretzels in a large bowl.
3. Break pretzels into pieces, as small as possible.
4. Stir pieces into the mixture until well saturated.
5. Place on a jellyroll pan and bake for 10 minutes.
6. Cool and store in a covered container.

Artichoke Dip

Serves 6 to 8

Scrumptious.

1 can artichoke hearts packed in salt water, drained
1 cup mayonnaise
1 cup Parmesan cheese, grated

Hint: Separates if heated in microwave oven. Use standard oven to prepare.

1. Preheat oven to 350°.
2. Chop up artichoke hearts.
3. Add mayonnaise and Parmesan cheese.
4. Spoon mixture into an ovenproof dish.
5. Bake for 20 minutes.
6. Serve with club crackers.

Shrimp Sparklers

Serves 6 to 8

"Finger Food" — easy to prepare and lots of fun to eat!

48 large shrimp
1 cup (2 sticks) butter
2 tablespoons Chesapeake Bay
　OR Cajun Seafood Seasoning

1. Wash and clean shrimp, removing legs only. Do not remove shells. (The shells hold in the spicy flavor of the seasoned butter.)

2. In large frypan melt butter over medium heat. Add seasoning. Stir to blend.

3. Place shrimp (with shells) into the simmering seasoned butter. Sauté until they turn coral pink.

4. Remove shrimp and place in large bowl. Pour remaining seasoned butter into individual bowls.

5. To eat, peel the shell and dip in the seasoned butter.

Serve with Sourdough bread.
Have lots of napkins handy and bowls for shells.

Star Spangled Salad Mold

Serves 6

Tastes as good as it looks!

2 4-ounce packages strawberry gelatin
2 cups water
1 10-ounce package frozen
　strawberries, thawed
½ cup sour cream
1½ cups miniature marshmallows
½ cup heavy cream, whipped
1 cup blueberries.

You can also use raspberry gelatin and frozen raspberries.

1. Dissolve gelatin in 2 cups boiling water. Chill until thickened.

2. Stir in thawed strawberries.

3. Pour into a 5-cup star mold. Mixture will fill mold about halfway. Chill until set.

4. Combine sour cream and marshmallows. Mix well.

5. Fold in whipped cream.

6. Unmold gelatin onto platter.

7. Frost top with marshmallow mixture; cover with blueberries.

8. Cover and refrigerate until ready to serve.

Marinated Carrots

Serves 6

1 pound carrots
1 lemon
3 tablespoons olive oil
½ teaspoon fennel seeds
¼ teaspoon hot red pepper flakes
½ teaspoon salt

Must be made the night before.

1. Peel carrots and grate into bowl.
2. Squeeze 2 tablespoons juice from the lemon.
3. Combine lemon juice, oil, fennel, pepper flakes and salt.
4. Pour over carrots and toss.
5. Cover and refrigerate overnight.

Pineapple Poultry Pasta

Serves 6 to 8

2 cups cooked chicken
1 8-ounce box pasta shells, cooked, drained and cooled
2 tablespoons crushed pineapple
2 teaspoons soy sauce
¼ cup green pepper, chopped
1 teaspoon scallions OR onions, finely chopped
½ cup mayonnaise
dash of ginger
½ cup pecans

1. In a large bowl, combine all ingredients.
2. Toss gently and thoroughly.
3. Chill until ready to serve. Will keep in refrigerator for several days.

Wild Rice And Cucumber Salad

Serves 8

1 1-pound box wild rice mix
¾ cup cucumbers, seeds removed and diced
½ cup celery, chopped
¾ cup cherry tomatoes, halved
⅓ cup mayonnaise
⅓ cup plain yogurt
½ teaspoon black pepper

1. Cook rice according to package directions, omitting butter.
2. Combine cucumbers, celery, tomatoes, mayonnaise, yogurt and pepper.
3. Add vegetable mixture to rice and stir well.

Chili Zeppieri

Serves 6 to 8

Spicy hot!

3 medium onions, chopped
2 cloves garlic, crushed
2 tablespoons salad oil
2 pounds ground beef
1 28-ounce can tomatoes, undrained
1 6-ounce can tomato paste
1 4-ounce can chopped green chilies
3 tablespoons chili powder
1 tablespoon ground cumin
1 bay leaf
2½ teaspoons salt
6 whole cloves
¼ teaspoon cayenne pepper
2 15-ounce cans red kidney beans, drained

1. In a large stockpot sauté onions and garlic in salad oil, about 5 minutes, until tender.
2. Add ground beef and cook until browned. Spoon off fat.
3. Add tomatoes, tomato paste, chilies and seasonings. Simmer, covered, over low heat for 2 hours, stirring occasionally.
4. Add drained beans and cook until just heated through.

Curry Explosion Chicken

Serves 4 to 6

A wonderful melding of flavors.

1 pound chicken breasts,
  cut into 1-inch cubes
1 tablespoon olive oil
1 green pepper, chopped
1 large onion, chopped
2 to 3 cloves garlic, crushed
1 green apple, peeled and chopped
½ cup raisins
½ cup sliced almonds
½ teaspoon pepper
½ teaspoon basil
1 tablespoon curry powder
½ teaspoon cayenne pepper
¼ teaspoon white pepper
1 15-ounce can stewed tomatoes
½ cup water

1. In a frypan sauté chicken in olive oil until cooked. Remove from pan.
2. Sauté pepper, onion and garlic. When almost done, add apples, raisins and almonds.
3. Return chicken to pan.
4. Add spices, tomatoes and water.
5. Simmer 30 minutes, stirring occasionally to blend ingredients.

Serve hot over boiled white rice.

Paella Peregrina

Serves 4 to 6

Delicioso!

4 boneless chicken breasts, cut in half
3 onions, chopped
½ cup oil
1 clove garlic, crushed
1 green pepper, chopped
1 red pepper, half chopped,
　half cut in strips
4 inches chorizo or pepperoni sausage,
　cut into half round slices
1 tablespoon salt
3 tablespoons parsley
saffron
1 pound shrimp, uncooked
1 cup frozen peas OR green beans,
　thawed
1½ cups yellow or long grain rice

Variables: Choose at least 2 of the following:

1 pound squid, cleaned and cut into circles
1 pound boneless fish fillet,
　cut into 2-inch squares
1 package or can of artichokes
8 to 10 fresh mussels or clams, scrubbed
1 lobster tail, cut into 2-inch chunks

**Instead of fresh seafood, substitute 1 can EACH
of clams, squid, or octopus if needed.**

1. Place chicken in a 2½-quart pan and cover with water. Add ½ onion. Cover and boil 20 minutes.

2. In 14-inch frypan with cover, large cast iron pot, or paelleria, heat ½ cup oil. Add garlic, remaining onions, green pepper, red pepper and sausage. Fry, covered, for 15 minutes.

3. Remove red pepper strips and save for decoration.

4. Measure 2½ cups of chicken broth from chicken pot and pour into frypan. (If not enough add water.) Set chicken pieces aside and cover to keep warm.

5. Add salt, parsley and a pinch of saffron. Bring to a hard boil.

6. Add the rest of the ingredients: shrimp, peas, squid, fish, artichokes, mussels, clams, lobster, etc. Let it boil hard 5 minutes.

7. Remove seafood and set aside with chicken. Keep warm.

8. Add rice to remaining liquid and continue to boil another 5 minutes.

9. Lower heat. Push pieces of chicken under rice. Arrange seafood and strips of red pepper on top to decorate.

10. Cover frypan and simmer 15 to 20 minutes or until rice is soft. If rice hasn't absorbed all liquid, leave cover off for a few more minutes.

11. Serve paella in frypan. Let guests help themselves.

Spicy Picnic Chicken

Serves 6

Delectable and aromatic.

2 cloves garlic, crushed
2½ teaspoons fresh ginger, minced
1½ teaspoons cumin
1½ teaspoons coriander, ground
¾ teaspoon tumeric
½ teaspoon cayenne pepper
1½ teaspoons salt
1½ cups plain yogurt
2 3-pound chickens

Requires some advance preparation.

1. Combine garlic, ginger, cumin, coriander, tumeric, cayenne, salt and yogurt.
2. Cut along one side of backbone of each chicken and then along the other to remove bone.
3. Spread chickens out and press down on breast bones to flatten.
4. Put chicken in large bowl.
5. Cover with yogurt marinade.
6. Refrigerate overnight.
7. Preheat oven to 350°.
8. Remove chicken from marinade, shake off excess.
9. Place on broiler rack.
10. Bake 45 to 50 minutes. Then broil 5 to 10 minutes to brown.
11. Let cool before packing for picnic.

Rockets Julienne

Serves 4 to 6

1 18x18-inch piece heavy duty foil
2 carrots
1 red pepper
1 zucchini
1 yellow squash
1 medium onion
1 tablespoon oil
1 tablespoon water
½ teaspoon salt
¼ teaspoon pepper
½ teaspoon garlic powder
½ teaspoon cumin
1 tablespoon butter

1. Preheat oven to 350°.
2. Cut all vegetables into thin strips and place in heavy duty foil.
3. Sprinkle vegetables with oil, water and seasonings. Dot with butter.
4. Fold foil over vegetables and fold edges to seal.
5. Bake for 30 minutes.
6. Take with you, as is, to picnic.

Can be served hot or at room temperature.
Variation: Wrap raw vegetables in foil and cook over hot coals or open fire.

Oriental Eggplant

Serves 4 to 6

1 large eggplant
2 tablespoons salt
1 teaspoon fresh ginger, grated
1 tablespoon red chile paste with garlic
1 tablespoon rice wine OR dry sherry
1 tablespoon light soy sauce
1 tablespoon hot bean sauce
1 tablespoon sweet bean sauce
3 cloves garlic, crushed
3 tablespoons peanut oil
4 scallions, chopped
1 tablespoons toasted sesame oil
3 scallion tops (greens) for garnish

Ingredients can be found in oriental food stores and larger supermarkets.

1. Cut stem off eggplant and cut into ¾-inch slices. Cut the slices again to make ¾-inch cubes.

2. In large bowl mix eggplant with salt.

3. Place in colander and drain for 45 minutes. Rinse and drain for another 45 minutes.

4. In a small bowl, mix ginger, chile paste, wine, soy sauce, hot bean sauce and sweet bean sauce. Stir and set aside.

5. Sauté garlic in peanut oil in wok or large frypan.

6. Add eggplant and scallions. Stir fry over high heat until the eggplant is tender (7 to 10 minutes).

7. Add sauce mixture and continue cooking for another 3 minutes.

8. Place on serving platter and drizzle sesame oil over the top. Add scallion greens for garnish.

Sourdough Bread

Makes 2 loaves

Sourdough Starter (makes 2 cups):

1 package dry yeast
½ cup warm water
2 cups flour
1 teaspoon salt
3 tablespoons sugar
2 cups warm water

Sourdough Starter may be frozen. Before using, let thaw at room temperature until mixture is bubbly (about 6 hours).

Starter preparation:

1. In a small bowl, dissolve yeast in ½ cup warm water. Let sit 5 minutes.

2. In a large glass bowl, combine flour, salt, sugar and 2 cups warm water.

3. Add yeast mixture and mix well.

4. Cover loosely with cheesecloth and let sit in a warm place (80°) for 72 hours, stirring 2 to 3 times daily.

5. Place fermented mixture in refrigerator and stir once daily; use within 10 days.

Starter Food:

½ cup sugar
1 cup flour
1 cup milk

Sourdough Bread:

1 cup milk, scalded
¼ cup (½ stick) butter
2 tablespoons sugar
6 cups flour, divided
1 tablespoon salt
2 packages dry yeast
1 cup Sourdough Starter

6. To use, remove Sourdough Starter from refrigerator and let sit at room temperature at least 1 hour.

7. Stir Starter and measure amount needed for recipe.

8. Replenish Starter with Starter Food (below), and use within 2 to 10 days, stirring daily.

9. When Sourdough Starter is used again, repeat procedure for using and replenishing Starter.

Starter Food preparation:

1. Stir all ingredients into remaining Sourdough Starter, and refrigerate.

Bread preparation:

1. In a medium saucepan, scald milk.

2. Add butter and sugar to milk. Stir until sugar is dissolved. Cool to lukewarm (110°).

3. In a large bowl, combine 3 cups flour with salt.

4. Add yeast, 1 cup Sourdough Starter, and milk mixture. Beat with electric mixer until mixture is smooth.

5. Cover and let rise in a warm place, 1 hour, until doubled in bulk.

6. Punch dough down and gradually work in remaining 3 cups flour to make a soft dough.

7. Divide dough in half. Roll each half into a rectangle 8x6 inches.

8. Starting at the widest end, roll up jellyroll fashion. Fold ends under and place in 2 well greased 9x5x3-inch bread pans.

9. Cover and let rise in a warm place, 1½ hours, until doubled in bulk.

10. Preheat oven to 350°.

11. When breads have doubled in bulk, bake for 40 minutes, until loaves sound hollow when tapped.

Italian Onion Bread — Focaccia   Serves 8

Can be used as a sandwich bread with meat between pieces.

1 package quick-rise yeast
1 teaspoon salt
2 cups flour
4 tablespoons olive oil
1 cup water
1 cup whole wheat flour
1 tablespoon cornmeal
1 medium red onion, sliced
2 tablespoons Parmesan cheese
1 tablespoon fresh rosemary
  OR 1 teaspoon dried rosemary
¼ teaspoon black pepper, cracked
½ teaspoon coarse salt (optional)
¼ cup dried tomatoes in oil,
  thinly sliced (optional)

1. About 2 hours before serving or early in the day, in a large bowl, combine yeast, salt and 1 cup flour.

2. In a 1-quart saucepan over medium heat, heat 2 tablespoons olive oil and 1 cup water until very warm (125° to 130°).

3. With mixer at low speed beat oil and water into yeast mixture until blended. Increase speed to medium; beat 2 minutes.

4. Add ½ cup more of flour, beat 2 minutes Stir in whole wheat flour. Knead dough about 8 minutes, working in remaining ½ cup flour. Cover and let rest 15 minutes.

5. Grease a 13x9-inch pan and sprinkle with cornmeal. Pat dough into pan, pushing well into corners. Cover, let rise in a warm place until doubled, about 30 minutes.

6. In a 2-quart saucepan, over medium heat, cook onion in 1 tablespoon of olive oil until tender. Set aside.

7. Preheat oven to 400°. With finger, make deep indentations over entire surface of dough; drizzle with 1 tablespoon olive oil; top with onion, Parmesan, rosemary, pepper, and if you like, coarse salt.

8. Bake bread 20 to 25 minutes until golden. Sprinkle with dried tomato.

Serve hot or cold.

Red, White and Blue Shortcake Serves 8

3 pints fresh strawberries
1 pint fresh blueberries
½ cup seedless raspberry jam
¼ cup Chambord liqueur
2 tablespoons sugar
whipped cream

1. Wash strawberries and blueberries. Remove stems and hulls. Select best strawberries and slice them. Reserve any of white ends and less perfect strawberries. Combine blueberries and strawberry slices in a large bowl.
2. In a food processor purée less perfect strawberries and white ends. Add jam, liqueur and sugar.
3. Add purée to fruit in bowl and refrigerate.
4. Serve with Shortcakes and whipped cream.

Shortcakes:

4 cups flour
6 tablespoons sugar
5 teaspoons baking powder
2 teaspoons salt
¾ cup butter, chilled
   and cut up in pieces
1½ cups heavy cream
3 tablespoons butter, melted

Shortcake preparation:

1. Preheat oven to 450°.
2. Sift flour, sugar, baking powder and salt together in a large bowl.
3. Add the butter and mix with your fingertips until it resembles coarse meal.
4. Add heavy cream and mix thoroughly until a soft dough forms.
5. Gather dough into a ball and knead it on a lightly floured surface. Roll out until about ¾-inch thick.
6. Cut out 8 3-inch circles and 8 2½-inch circles. Put 3-inch circles on lightly buttered cookie sheet. Brush tops with melted butter.
7. Place 2½-inch circles on top of 3-inch circles.
8. Bake in middle of oven 12 to 15 minutes until golden brown and firm to the touch.

Serve WARM with fruit and whipped cream.

Chocolate Mousse

Serves 6

12 ounces semi-sweet chocolate chips
4 eggs, separated
2 whole eggs
2 teaspoons vanilla
2 cups heavy cream
2 teaspoons confectioner's sugar
6 strawberries (optional)

An easy way to melt chocolate: Bring water to boil in the bottom of the double boiler. Place top of double boiler over bottom. Add chocolate, cover and turn off heat. Let sit for 8 minutes. Remove cover and stir. Chocolate will be melted.

1. Melt the chocolate in a double boiler. Remove the melted chocolate from the heat and let cool.
2. Separate the whites from the yolks of four eggs. Place whites in a small bowl and yolks in a medium bowl.
3. Beat the four yolks together with two whole eggs. Stir in cooled melted chocolate.
4. Beat the four egg whites with an electric mixer until soft peaks form.
5. Gently fold the egg whites into the chocolate mixture.
6. In a separate bowl whip ¾ cup of the heavy cream. Fold it into the chocolate mixture. Pour the mixture into 6 individual dessert bowls and refrigerate for at least 2 hours.
7. When mousse is firm, whip the rest of the heavy cream. Stir the vanilla and sugar into the whipped cream.
8. Put a dollop of whipped cream on top of each serving of mousse. Top each with a strawberry and serve.

Grand Finale Pie

Serves 8 to 10

Green tomatoes provide a spectacular ending!

6 green tomatoes
1½ cups sugar
pastry for double-crust pie
½ lemon, rind and all
¼ teaspoon salt
¼ cup flour
¼ teaspoon cinnamon
¼ teaspoon ginger

1. Preheat oven to 425°.
2. Line the bottom of a 9-inch pie plate with pastry.
3. Slice the tomatoes very thin (round ⅛-inch slices).
4. Put ¾ cup of the sugar on the bottom of prepared crust.
5. Add the tomatoes.

6. Cut the lemon into small shavings and sprinkle over tomatoes.

7. Combine salt, flour, remaining ¾ cup sugar and the spices. Sprinkle over tomatoes.

8. Cover with top crust and bake 10 minutes at 425°. Reduce heat to 350° and continue baking for 40.

Lynn Anderson's Salsa

Makes 1 quart

Can be eaten with everything: chips, barbecued meat, hamburgers and hot dogs.

1 16-ounce can whole tomatoes, OR
  6 to 8 fresh tomatoes, roasted and peeled
1 medium onion, chopped
3 cloves garlic, crushed
6 to 12 Mexican peppers (your choice of
  any combination of jalapeño, Serrano,
  Poblano, yellow, etc.)
1 teaspoon cilantro (coriander), chopped
¼ teaspoon salt

1. Chop all ingredients and throw them together in a bowl and that's it.

Use all 12 peppers for the hottest salsa.

Orange Pineapple Punch

Makes 16 8-ounce servings

Caution: Easy to drink but packs a whallop!

1 cup pineapple juice
2 cups orange juice
6 lemons, juiced
¾ cup confectioner's sugar
6 ounces Cointreau liqueur
1 quart vodka
2 quarts ginger ale

1. Combine pineapple juice, orange juice, juice of lemons, sugar, Contreau liqueur and vodka.

2. Pour over ice in a thermal jug.

3. Add ginger ale to glasses when serving.

If serving at home, pour all ingredients over an ice ring in punch bowl.

LOVE ON THE RUN

EXECUTIVE OFFICER

127

SAMPLE MENU

White Wine Love Potion

True Love Salad

"Hearty" Pasta Salad

Cupid's Biscuits

Sweetie Pies

Chocolate Kisses

Tea for Two

In our hectic, harried world we need time to share a bite (and kisses), or lunch (and kisses), or dinner (and kisses) with someone we love. So we've come up with some recipes for amorous table treats. You might choose to spirit your sweetheart away for a surprise picnic on a gloomy Monday. If you work in separate locations, you might meet in the middle with a gourmet offering for each other. The possibilities for rendezvous are endless. Whatever the setting, we've tried to help with food ideas. Guaranteed to garner heartfelt appreciation *and kisses.*

Avocado Bacon Boats

Serves 6

12 slices bacon
½ cup sour cream
2 tomatoes, peeled, seeded
  and finely chopped
2 tablespoons onion, finely chopped
1 tablespoon lemon juice
¼ teaspoon salt
3 avocados, halved and pitted

1. Cook bacon until crisp. Remove to paper
   towel, cool and crumble.
2. Mix bacon, sour cream, tomato, onion,
   lemon juice and salt.
3. Scoop out avocado halves. Dice meat.
4. Fold avocado into sour cream mixture.
   Spoon into avocado shells.

Cucumber and Sour Cream Salad   Serves 4 to 6

4 cucumbers
¼ cup fresh dill, finely chopped
2 tablespoons white wine vinegar
1 cup sour cream
½ teaspoon salt
¼ teaspoon pepper

1. Peel cucumbers, slice thin and place
   in bowl.
2. Add dill, vinegar, sour cream, salt
   and pepper.
3. Toss lightly and marinate 1 hour.
4. Drain slightly and serve cold.

Mushroom Salad

Serves 4 to 6

3 tablespoons scallions, thinly sliced
1 tablespoon Dijon mustard
½ cup olive oil
1½ tablespoons wine vinegar
1 teaspoon sugar
1 teaspoon garlic powder
½ teaspoon salt
¼ teaspoon pepper
1 pound mushrooms, thinly sliced

1. Whisk together scallions, mustard, olive
   oil, vinegar, sugar and garlic powder until
   lightly thickened.
2. Add salt and pepper.
3. Pour over mushrooms and chill until
   ready to serve.

True Love Salad

Serves 4

A marriage of fruit and cheese.

1 head bibb lettuce
2 ripe pears, sliced
¼ pound Gorgonzola cheese, crumbled
¼ cup raspberry vinaigrette dressing

1. Tear lettuce into pieces and place
   in salad bowl.
2. Add pears and cheese.
3. Toss with dressing and serve.

Orange Wild Rice Salad

Serves 6 to 8

5 cups water
1 cup wild rice
1 cup brown rice
½ cup pine nuts, toasted
4 tablespoons Italian parsley, chopped
2 tablespoons orange rind, grated
¼ cup olive oil
2 tablespoons orange juice,
  freshly squeezed
1 teaspoon salt
½ teaspoon pepper

1. Preheat oven to 350°.
2. Bring 3 cups of water to a boil and add wild rice. Stir, reduce heat, cover and simmer 25 minutes. Drain.
3. Bring 2 cups of water to a boil and add brown rice. Simmer 15 minutes. Drain.
4. In a large bowl toss wild and brown rices together.
5. Add pine nuts, parsley, orange rind, olive oil and orange juice. Mix well.
6. Add salt and pepper. Mix thoroughly.
7. Place mixture in a casserole dish. Cover and bake 30 minutes.

Serve hot or cold.

"Hearty" Pasta Salad

Serves 4 to 6

For seafood lovers.

1 pound heart shaped pasta*
1 pound seafood, (any combination
  of shrimp, scallops, crab or lobster)
1 red pepper, chopped
2 carrots, thinly sliced
1 cup green beans, sliced diagonally

* Available at gourmet or specialty food stores

Lemon Vinaigrette:
⅓ cup fresh lemon juice
1 cup olive oil
1 large clove garlic, crushed
2 tablespoons white wine
¼ cup fresh parsley, chopped
¼ cup scallions, shallots or chives, chopped
½ teaspoon salt
¼ teaspoon pepper

1. Cook pasta according to package directions. Drain and set aside.
2. Clean seafood and cook as desired. Let cool and cut into bite size pieces. Place in large bowl and set aside.
3. In a large pot of boiling water, blanch red pepper, carrots and green beans for 2 minutes. Drain and cool.
4. Add cooked pasta and vegetables to bowl with seafood.
5. Add lemon vinaigrette and toss gently. Cover and chill for several hours.

Lemon Vinaigrette preparation:

1. Combine lemon juice, oil, garlic, wine, parsley, scallions, salt and pepper. Mix well.

Fruity Chicken Pasta Salad

Serves 6 to 8

A wonderful summer salad for dinner guests.

3 whole chicken breasts, cooked, boned
   and cut into small pieces
1 1-pound package twist pasta, cooked
2 cups seedless grapes, halved
1 1-pound can mandarin oranges, drained
1 kiwi, peeled and sliced
1 cup snow peas
2 stalks celery, chopped
½ cucumber sliced and quartered
½ cup raisins
1 scallion, chopped
spinach or lettuce leaves
   to line salad bowl

1. Toss all ingredients together with Dressing, leaving a few grapes, oranges, kiwi and snow peas to decorate top.
2. Place in a large bowl lined with spinach leaves or lettuce leaves.
3. Cover and refrigerate until ready to serve. (Can sit for several hours.)

Dressing:

⅔ cup mayonnaise
½ cup Parmesan cheese
⅓ cup fresh lemon juice
½ teaspoon salt
¼ teaspoon pepper

Dressing preparation:

1. Beat all ingredients together and pour over salad.

Chicken Tenders Pizza

Serves 4 to 6

A very different pizza.

8 ounces pizza dough
½ cup of your favorite barbecue sauce
¼ cup smoked Gouda cheese, shredded
¼ cup Mozzarella cheese, shredded
1 8-ounce package chicken tenders, cubed
¼ cup red onion, chopped
¼ cup cilantro (coriander), chopped

1. Preheat oven to 400°.
2. Roll and stretch dough to fit a 12-inch round pizza pan.
3. Spread barbecue sauce over dough.
4. In a bowl mix Gouda and Mozzarella and sprinkle half of the mixture on sauce.
5. Place chicken tenders on top of cheeses.
6. Sprinkle red onion and cilantro over chicken.
7. Sprinkle remaining cheese mixture on top to cover ingredients.
8. Bake for 15 to 20 minutes until cheese is lightly browned.

Turkey And Spinach Meatloaf

Serves 4 to 6

Easy to make, very tasty, and even low-fat!

1 8-ounce package frozen chopped spinach, thawed
1 pound ground turkey
1 egg
¾ cup bread crumbs
½ cup onion, chopped
   OR 2 tablespoons onion flakes
1 tablespoon parsley
2 teaspoons lemon juice
3 tablespoons ketchup
dash of soy sauce (optional)
½ teaspoon salt
¼ teaspoon pepper
¼ cup skim milk to moisten

Can be served with a cream sauce.

1. Preheat oven to 350°.
2. In a large bowl mix spinach with turkey, egg, bread crumbs, onion, parsley, lemon juice, ketchup, soy sauce, salt and pepper.
3. Gradually moisten with skim milk and form loaf.
4. Place in a 5x9-inch loaf pan and cover loosely with foil.
5. Bake 1 hour.
6. Cool 5 to 10 minutes before slicing.

Freezes well.

Baked Stuffed Shrimp

Serves 4

Elegant yet easy to prepare.

12 jumbo shrimp
½ cup (1 stick) butter
2 tablespoons garlic, crushed
1 roll of buttery flavored crackers, crushed
½ cup parsley, finely chopped
3 tablespoons lemon juice
2 tablespoons Parmesan cheese, grated

1. Clean, devein and remove shells from shrimp, leaving on tails. Spread open to stuff.
2. Melt butter in medium saucepan. Add garlic and sauté on low heat until soft. Remove from heat.
3. Stir in crackers, parsley, lemon juice and Parmesan cheese.
4. Stuff each shrimp with cracker mixture and place in an ovenproof serving dish.
5. Refrigerate. When ready to serve bake at 350° for 15 to 20 minutes.

Time varies with size of shrimp.

This family recipe is served each year for Christmas dinner. Prepare ahead, refrigerate and then bake when guests arrive.

Southern Cornbread Casserole   Serves 6 to 8

Cornbread:

1 10-ounce package cornbread mix
1 8¾-ounce can cream-style corn
1½ cups Swiss cheese, shredded
2 eggs, slightly beaten
2 tablespoons milk
2 teaspoons prepared mustard
1 14-ounce can artichoke hearts,
  drained and chopped
1 3-ounce can chopped
  mushrooms, drained

Cornbread preparation:

1. Preheat oven to 350°.
2. Grease an 8-inch square baking dish.
3. In a medium bowl, combine cornbread mix, corn, ½ cup cheese, eggs, milk and mustard.
4. Spread about 1 cup of this batter in the baking dish.
5. In a medium bowl, mix artichokes, mushrooms and remaining 1 cup cheese.
6. Spoon over batter in baking dish.
7. Top with remaining batter.
8. Bake 35 minutes or until cornbread is golden brown and has pulled away from sides of dish.
9. Let stand 10 minutes before cutting into squares.
10. To serve, ladle Southern Cream Sauce (below) over individual cornbread squares.

Southern Cream Sauce:

2 tablespoons butter
2 tablespoons flour
¾ cup chicken broth
¾ cup half-and-half
2 egg yolks, slightly beaten
1 cup chicken or turkey, cubed
1 cup ham, cubed

Sauce preparation:

1. In a medium saucepan, melt butter over medium heat.
2. Blend in flour and stir.
3. Add chicken broth and half-and-half. Stir constantly over medium heat until sauce thickens and bubbles.
4. Blend ¾ cup of sauce into beaten egg yolks, mix well.
5. Add egg yolk mixture to hot sauce. Stir in chicken and ham. Stir constantly over medium heat until heated through. Keep warm.

Vegetable Timbales

Serves 6 to 8

Well worth the time.

2 cups vegetable of your choice, puréed
1 teaspoon salt
½ teaspoon pepper
4 eggs, beaten
1½ cup half-and-half OR light cream
¼ cup onion, chopped
¼ cup cheddar cheese, grated
dash nutmeg

1. Preheat oven to 375°.
2. Purée vegetable of your choice (see variations and directions below.)
3. Generously butter 6 5-ounce ramekins or 8 4½-ounce timbale molds, or custard cups. Butter pieces of foil to cover each mold.
4. Stir 2 cups of vegetable purée into heavy saucepan and heat over low heat until liquid evaporates, about 5 minutes. Remove from heat and cool 5 minutes. Beat in remaining ingredients until smooth. Pour into prepared ramekins. Cover each with buttered foil and put into roasting pan and transfer to preheated oven. Add enough boiling water to come halfway up the sides of molds.
5. Bake until custards are set, about 35 to 40 minutes. DO NOT LET WATER BOIL. Add cold water should this happen. Cool 5 minutes and run knife around edge of mold. Invert onto dish. Can be served with a sauce (tomato, béchamel, hollandaise). If so, pour 2 to 3 tablespoons of sauce around the base of each timbale.

Variations:

BROCCOLI: Peel 2 pounds broccoli and cut into small pieces. Boil in salted water until tender, about 3 minutes. Chill in cold water and drain well. Process in food processor until very smooth.

SPINACH: Steam 4 pounds or 2 10-ounce packages frozen spinach. Squeeze dry and process in food processor until very smooth.

CARROTS: Peel and slice 2 pounds of carrots and boil until tender. Chill in cold water and drain well. Process in food processor until very smooth.

Cupid's Biscuits

This vintage recipe will steal your heart.

4 cups flour
2 tablespoons baking powder
I cup (2 sticks) butter
I½ to I¾ cups buttermilk

Terrific as an hors d'oeuvre: Make I½-inch in diameter and serve with country ham and French mustard.

Makes 2 dozen

1. Preheat oven to 450°.
2. Grease baking sheet.
3. Stir flour and baking powder in medium mixing bowl.
4. Cut butter into flour mixture using pastry blender.
5. Add buttermilk and thoroughly blend. Dough should be slightly wet and sticky.
6. Lightly flour counter and roll out dough to ½-inch thickness.
7. Add flour (lightly sprinkled) to top of dough as needed to prevent sticking to rolling pin.
8. Cut biscuits 2½ inches in diameter (I½ inches if using as cocktail biscuits).
9. Place on cookie sheet and bake for I2 minutes, until tops are golden brown. Biscuits will have a crunchy crust and light, fluffy interior.

Biscuits will more than double in height when baking. Recipe may be cut in half.

Stuffed Strawberry Muffins

So delectable with a surprise inside.

I⅔ cups flour
½ cup sugar
2 teaspoons baking powder
½ teaspoon salt
¼ teaspoon nutmeg OR cinnamon
¾ cup milk
I egg beaten
⅓ cup butter, melted
¼ cup strawberry jam

Makes I2 muffins

1. Preheat oven to 400°. Grease muffin pan.
2. Combine dry ingredients in medium bowl.
3. Combine milk, egg and butter. Gently stir into dry ingredients until moistened.
4. Spoon batter into greased pan (reserving ½ cup for tops). Put one teaspoon of strawberry filling in each muffin.
5. Spoon remaining batter on top of strawberry jam and bake for I5 to 20 minutes.
6. Remove muffins from pan and cool on wire rack.

Buttery Pound Cake

Serves 8 to 10

Extremely rich!

1 cup (2 sticks) butter
2 cups sugar
4 eggs
3 cups flour
1 teaspoon baking powder
1 teaspoon baking soda
½ teaspoon salt
1 cup buttermilk
2 teaspoons vanilla

1. Preheat oven to 350°.
2. Grease and flour Bundt or tube pan.
3. In a medium bowl cream butter and sugar.
4. Beat in eggs, one at a time. Set aside.
5. In a large bowl combine flour, baking powder, baking soda and salt.
6. Stir in buttermilk and vanilla. Mix well.
7. Add creamed mixture and mix thoroughly.
8. Pour into prepared pan and bake 1 hour.
9. Remove cake from oven when done and prick top with fork.
10. Slowly pour sauce over top and allow to soak into cake.
11. Cool cake in pan on wire rack. Remove when cooled.

Sauce:

½ cup (1 stick) butter.
¼ cup water
1 cup sugar
2 teaspoons vanilla

Sauce preparation:

1. In a small saucepan melt butter. Add water, sugar and vanilla and stir until well blended.

Chocolate Pecan Pie

Serves 8 to 10

Two loves in one.

4 eggs
½ cup sugar
½ cup light corn syrup
½ cup (1 stick) butter, melted
1 teaspoon bourbon
1 cup chocolate chips
2 cups pecans
1 prepared 8- or 9-inch pie crust

1. Preheat oven to 350°.
2. In a large bowl beat together eggs and sugar.
3. In a separate bowl mix together corn syrup, butter and bourbon. Add to egg mixture.
4. Sprinkle chips and nuts into crust.
5. Pour the prepared mixture over chips and nuts.
6. Bake 30 minutes.

Whoopie Pies

Makes 2 dozen

Cake:

1 cup sugar
3 egg yolks
1 whole egg
½ cup (1 stick) butter, softened
1 teaspoon vanilla
1 cup buttermilk
  OR substitute 1 cup milk mixed
  with 1 tablespoon vinegar and
  allow to stand for 5 minutes
2 cups flour
1 teaspoon baking powder
1 teaspoon baking soda
½ teaspoon salt
¼ cup cocoa

Filling:

¾ cup (1½ sticks) butter
1⅓ cups confectioner's sugar
half a 7-ounce jar of marshmallow creme
½ teaspoon vanilla

Cake preparation:

1. Preheat oven to 350°.
2. In a large bowl cream together the sugar, egg yolks, egg, butter, vanilla and buttermilk.
3. Into a small bowl sift flour, baking powder, baking soda, salt and cocoa.
4. Add sifted ingredients to creamed ingredients and mix thoroughly.
5. Drop by heaping tablespoonfuls onto greased cookie sheet.
6. Bake 15 to 20 minutes.
7. Cool on wire rack.

Filling preparation:

1. Beat all filling ingredients together until smooth.
2. Spread 1 tablespoon filling on one cooled cake.
3. Cover with second cake.
4. Repeat with other cakes.

Sweetie Pies

Serves 8

Crust:

2 cups graham crackers, crushed
½ cup almonds, finely chopped
¼ cup (½ stick) butter, melted
2 tablespoons honey
½ teaspoon cinnamon

Crust preparation:

1. Preheat oven to 300°.
2. Mix graham crackers with almonds, butter, honey and cinnamon.
3. Press firmly into 8 3-inch individual tart pans.
4. Bake for 10 minutes.
5. Cool in pans on wire rack.

Filling:

12 ounces cream cheese, softened
½ cup sour cream
¼ cup honey
1 pound can cherry pie filling

Filling preparation:

1. Beat together cream cheese, sour cream and honey.
2. Spoon into cooled shells and spread to edges.
3. Chill for 3 hours.
4. Top with cherry pie filling.
5. Chill until ready to serve.

Pears In Red Wine

Serves 6 to 8

4 cups red wine
2 sticks cinnamon
1 cup sugar
dash ground cloves
2 tablespoons lemon juice
6 to 8 pears, peeled, halved and cored

1. Combine wine, cinnamon, sugar, cloves and lemon juice in a large saucepan. Bring to a simmer.
2. Add pear halves and cook 20 minutes until tender.
3. Cool and chill.

Fruity Champagne Punch

Makes 25 8-ounce servings

1 46-ounce can unsweetened
  pineapple juice, chilled
1 46-ounce can peach nectar, chilled
2 cups water
3 750 milliliter bottles champagne, chilled
1 orange, sliced
1 lemon, sliced

1. Stir together juice, nectar and water in punch bowl.
2. Add champagne.
3. Garnish with orange and lemon slices.

ON BOARD

SAMPLE MENU

Port and Starboard Sipper

Deep Sea Dip

One Pot Bermuda Race Special

Boatswain's Bread

Breezy Lemon Fluff

Along the coast, with "water, water, everywhere," boats and ships are familiar sights. Whether it be on a rubber raft or an elegant yacht, there are many opportunities to "go down to the sea again." Yet, unlike poet John Masefield, your deckhands may need more than "a tall ship and a star to steer her by." So, be sure the hold is stocked with seagoing surprises. All hands will quickly be on deck and eager to plunge right into the following recipes.

Deep Sea Dip

This is a favorite of Captain Herb.

1 8-ounce package cream cheese, softened
3 cloves garlic, crushed
1 teaspoon dried basil
1 teaspoon chives
1 teaspoon caraway seed
1 teaspoon dill
2 teaspoons dried parsley, crushed
⅛ teaspoon black pepper, freshly ground

Makes 1 cup

1. In a blender thoroughly mix all ingredients together.
2. Mold into any shape desired.
3. Cover and refrigerate overnight.
4. Unmold on a serving dish.

Serve with crackers and raw vegetables. Must be made ahead.

Sausage Whirls

1 pound hot bulk sausage
½ cup onion, chopped
1 tablespoon oil
2 cups flour
½ teaspoon salt
3 teaspoons baking powder
5 tablespoons butter
⅔ cup milk

Makes 40 pieces

1. In a large frypan sauté sausage and onion in 1 tablespoon oil until browned. Set aside.
2. In a large bowl combine flour, salt and baking powder.
3. Cut in butter with pastry blender until mixture resembles coarse crumbs.
4. Stir in milk to make soft dough.
5. Divide dough in half. Roll out each half on a floured surface making 2 10x15-inch rectangles ½-inch thick.
6. Spread evenly with sausage and onion.
7. Roll up as for jellyroll. Seal edges.
8. Wrap in plastic wrap and freeze until ready to use.
9. Thaw bread and preheat oven to 400°.
10. Bake "loaves" on greased baking sheet 10 minutes until golden.
11. Cool 10 minutes before slicing.

Serve warm.

Herring Paté

1 12-ounce jar herring in cream
  or wine sauce, drained
1 8-ounce package cream cheese
½ cup pitted ripe olives
⅓ cup fresh parsley, chopped
juice of half a lemon

Optional:
black olives
hard-boiled eggs

Makes 3 cups

1. Place all ingredients in a food processor
   and process at highest speed until smooth.
2. Put mixture into a crock; cover and chill.

**Serve on party rye bread slices with chopped
black olives and chopped hard-boiled eggs for
garnish, if desired.**

Cabbage Salad

½ head cabbage, shredded
4 scallions, sliced
¼ cup red or green pepper, sliced
½ cup toasted slivered almonds
2 tablespoons raw sunflower seeds
1 package chicken flavored
  Chinese noodles, cooked

Dressing:
¼ cup oil
1 tablespoon sesame oil
2 tablespoons sugar
3 tablespoons rice wine vinegar
1 tablespoon soy sauce
1 flavor packet from Chinese noodles

Serves 4

1. Combine all salad ingredients.
2. Whisk all dressing ingredients together.
3. When ready to serve, pour dressing over
   vegetables and toss.

Macaroni Salad

Serves 4 to 6

1 pound box small macaroni
1 cup olive oil
2/3 cup white wine vinegar
2 tablespoons dry basil
2 cloves garlic, crushed
2/3 cup Parmesan cheese, grated
1/4 teaspoon pepper
1/2 teaspoon salt
1/4 cup parsely
1 large green pepper, diced

1. Cook macaroni until just tender, 8 minutes. Rinse with cold water, drain and set aside.
2. In a large bowl mix remaining ingredients, except parsley and green pepper.
3. Add cooled macaroni and toss to coat.
4. Chill overnight or several hours.
5. One-half hour before serving, add parsley and green pepper and toss gently.

Requires some advance preparation.

Fennel Fish Soup

Serves 6 to 8

Similar to Connecticut Chowder (no milk or tomatoes).

Fish Stock:
4 quarts water
several fish heads, bones, etc.
2 cups fennel stems and greens
1 teaspoon salt
1/2 teaspoon pepper
1/2 teaspoon dill
1/2 teaspoon thyme

Fish Stock preparation:
1. In stockpot, pour 4 quarts water over fish stock ingredients.
2. Cook 30 minutes over medium heat.
3. Strain and *reserve 1 quart broth*.

Soup:
1 cup onions, chopped
2 cloves garlic, crushed
1 tablespoon olive oil
1 quart Fish Stock
2 medium potatoes, cubed
2 cups fennel bulb, chopped
1 teaspoon salt
1/2 teaspoon pepper
1 teaspoon Worcestershire sauce
1 pound whitefish (cod, haddock, catfish) cut into 1-inch pieces

Soup preparation:
1. In frypan, sauté onions and garlic in olive oil until translucent. Set aside.
2. Pour 1 quart fish stock into stock pot and add potatoes. Cook 20 minutes until tender. Mash coarsely.
3. Add cooked onions and garlic, fennel, salt, pepper, Worcestershire and fish.
4. Cook 15 to 20 minutes until fish is done.

Can be frozen.

Beef And Vegetable Soup

Serves 4 to 6

Cook and serve this "meal-in-one" soup in same container.

1½ pounds lean ground round
1 16-ounce can stewed tomatoes
2 5-ounce cans V8 juice
3 cups water
1 11-ounce can beef bouillon, undiluted
1 package dry onion soup mix
　(Sieve slightly to remove some of the
　seasonings)
1 tablespoon dark brown sugar
1 tablespoon basil
¼ teaspoon black pepper, ground
1 10-ounce package frozen mixed vegetables

**If you need to thin soup, use equal parts
of bouillon, V8 juice and water.**

1. In a non-metal pot over medium heat, lightly brown meat. Drain off fat.
2. Add tomatoes, juice, water, bouillon, onion soup mix, brown sugar, basil, pepper and mixed vegetables.
3. Bring to a boil, stirring occasionally.
4. Lower heat and simmer for 45 minutes to 1 hour, partially covered.
5. When cooked and cool, remove any fat, cover and refrigerate.

**Flavor improves if made a day ahead.
May be frozen if made in large quantity.**

**Created on a trip from Oxford, Maryland to Florida, this tasty soup
has become a family favorite. It's a complete meal and is easy to
make "on board."**

Tomato Bouillon

Serves 4 to 6

Complement to a sandwich lunch when on the water in the crisp air.

1 11-ounce can beef bouillon
1 11-ounce can beef consommé
3 cups tomato juice
6 whole cloves
6 whole peppercorns
1 tablespoon dry green onion flakes

1. In a large saucepan, simmer together undiluted bouillon consommé and tomato juice.
2. Add cloves, peppercorns and dry green onion flakes.
3. Simmer for at least 1 hour, covered.
4. Strain seasonings before serving in large mugs.

Serve the same day.

Sailor's Soup

Serves 12 sailors

2 pounds lean ground beef
2 large onions, chopped (2 to 3 cups)
2 cloves garlic, crushed
1½ pounds red potatoes, cubed
*½ cup turnips, chopped
*½ cup parsnips, chopped
*1 large green pepper, chopped
*1 cup celery, chopped
2 10-ounce cans tomato soup
2 10-ounce cans vegetarian vegetable soup
4 10-ounce cans of water
1 16-ounce bag frozen mixed vegetables
pepper, Tabasco and Worcestershire
   sauce to taste

*These items are optional.

Meat, onions and potatoes can be found in almost any port, but be sure to stock the soup on board.

1. Brown ground beef in a large pot.
2. Add onions and garlic, sauté 5 minutes.
3. Add all vegetables except frozen mixed vegetables.
4. Stir in canned soups and water.
5. Simmer 30 minutes, partially covered or until potatoes are almost done.
6. Add frozen vegetables. Add seasonings as desired. Simmer an additional 5 minutes.
7. Cool, pack in 1-quart containers and reheat on board as needed.

As with most soups and stews, this is more flavorful when made a day ahead.

My father grew up sailing and racing on the Great Lakes. He did day racing as well as long distance races such as the Port Huron-Mackinac. He always felt that a warm, nourishing meal made all the difference in a crew's morale and ability to win. In order for that to happen — the meal needed to be one dish and easy to prepare.

Crab Quiche

Serves 8

Low cal and low fat.

2 cups crabmeat, flaked
½ onion, finely chopped
1 cup low fat sharp
   cheddar cheese, grated
egg substitute to equal 3 eggs
1½ cups low fat milk
⅛ teaspoon salt

1. Preheat oven to 350°.
2. Line bottom of a 9-inch quiche dish or baking pan with crabmeat.
3. Sprinkle onion over crabmeat.
4. Sprinkle grated cheese on top.
5. Combine eggs, milk and salt. Mix well.
6. Pour over crabmeat mixture.
7. Bake 1 hour.
8. Allow to stand for 10 minutes before cutting into pie-shaped wedges or squares, depending on pan.

Pot Luck Stew

Serves 10 to 12

Similar to English Pot Pie without the crust.

4 pork chops
1 tablespoon oil
2 quarts chicken stock
1 to 2 tablespoons bottled brown sauce
2 large onions, chopped
4 large potatoes, peeled and quartered
¼ cup parsley, chopped
4 chicken breasts
4 chicken legs
1 pound of leftover pot roast,
  or steak, sliced
1½ cups leftover gravy
1½ cups carrots, cut into sticks
1½ cups green beans, whole
1½ cups yams, cut into long quarters
1½ cups broccoli, cut into 2-inch lengths
1½ cups red wine

1. In a large stockpot, over medium high heat, brown pork chops in oil. Add chicken stock, brown sauce, onions, potatoes, parsley and chicken pieces. Bring to a boil, lower heat and simmer for 45 to 60 minutes.
2. Add the cooked pot roast or steak and gravy and stir.
3. Add carrots, green beans, yams, broccoli and wine. Stir and simmer 10 minutes.

Can be served over homemade buttermilk biscuits.

Binky's Chicken

Serves 6 to 8

Avoid being a galley slave! Bake, freeze, take on board, and just reheat.

2 tablespoons butter
2 tablespoons olive oil
½ cup flour
1 teaspoon salt
½ teaspoon rosemary
4 whole boneless chicken breasts
½ cup apricot preserves
1 tablespoon Dijon mustard
½ cup plain yogurt

1. Melt butter and add olive oil in a 9x13-inch pan while preheating oven to 350°.
2. In a large self-locking plastic bag, combine flour, salt and rosemary.
3. Shake pieces of chicken in flour mixture.
4. Place chicken in pan with melted butter and olive oil.
5. Mix apricot preserves, mustard and yogurt.
6. Pour over chicken.
7. Bake for 45 minutes.

Serve hot or cold with rice or noodles.

One Pot Bermuda Race Special

Serves 8

Practically cooks itself while you tend the sails.

6 carrots, scraped and cut in 2-inch lengths
2 parsnips, scraped and cut in 2-inch lengths
4 large potatoes, peeled and quartered
2 celery stalks, sliced
2 onions, sliced
1 2-pound ham butt OR
  1 2-pound smoked boneless
  pork shoulder butt
1 head cabbage, separated into leaves

1. Layer all vegetables except cabbage in a large pot with a tight-fitting lid.
2. Place ham on top of vegetables.
3. Add 2 inches of water, and layer cabbage leaves over ham.
4. Cover pot and cook over medium heat for 1 hour or until potatoes are tender.
5. Check periodically to be sure water doesn't evaporate completely.
6. Serve hot with butter, salt and pepper.

Reuben Bake

Serves 4 to 6

1 8-ounce package egg noodles,
  cooked and drained
2 tablespoons butter, melted
1 16-ounce can sauerkraut, partially drained
½ teaspoon caraway seeds
⅛ teaspoon garlic powder
1 pound corned beef, thinly sliced
  and chopped
1 cup Russian or Thousand Island dressing
2 tomatoes, thinly sliced
2 cups Swiss cheese, shredded
½ cup rye crackers, crushed
2 tablespoons butter, melted
1 package buttermilk biscuits (optional)

1. Preheat oven to 350°.
2. Mix noodles with melted butter in a 9x13-inch casserole.
3. In a large bowl mix sauerkraut with caraway seeds and garlic powder. Spoon over noodles.
4. Place corned beef on top of sauerkraut.
5. Spread dressing over corned beef and arrange tomato slices over dressing.
6. Sprinkle with Swiss cheese.
7. In a small bowl mix crackers with 2 tablespoons butter and sprinkle as final layer.
8. Bake 35 minutes or until mixture is hot and bubbly.
9. Allow to sit 20 minutes before serving.

Can be topped with buttermilk biscuits and baked as directed.

'Kraut Pudding

½ pound sausage meat
1 small head of cabbage
2 eggs
⅛ teaspoon nutmeg
¼ teaspoon salt
scant cup bread crumbs

Serves 4 to 6

1. In a medium frypan brown sausage meat. Drain fat and set aside meat.
2. Remove and set aside 3 or 4 large outside leaves from cabbage head.
3. In a large stockpot boil remaining cabbage. Drain, finely chop and place in large bowl.
4. Add browned sausage, eggs, nutmeg, salt and bread crumbs. Mix thoroughly.
5. Line plum pudding mold with raw cabbage leaves saved earlier.
6. Pack cabbage/sausage mixture into mold and fold over leaf ends before covering with lid.
7. Cook on top of stove by setting mold into pot of simmering hot water and steam covered for 2 hours.
8. Serve by inverting kraut pudding onto serving platter, uncovering pudding by removing outer cabbage leaves.
9. Slice and serve.

**Top with medium white sauce.
Serve with mashed potatoes.**

Scallops Tarragon

1 pound sea scallops, washed and dried
3 tablespoons butter
⅓ cup white wine
½ teaspoon dry tarragon
   OR 1 teaspoon fresh tarragon

Serves 4

1. Melt butter over medium heat in frypan.
2. Add scallops. Cook for 1 minute.
3. Add wine and tarragon. Cook for 4 minutes.
4. Increase heat and cook 1 minute longer.

Serve hot with rice pilaf, garnished with lemon.

Shrimp Scampi "Osprey"

Serves 4

Served after a "heads up" sail to Greenport, L.I.

¼ cup olive oil
1 tablespoon garlic chips
½ cup dry white wine
juice of 1 lemon
1 teaspoon oregano
¼ teaspoon tarragon
1 teaspoon basil
1 pound fettucini
1 pound large fresh shrimp,
  deveined
¼ cup Parmesan cheese

1. Heat oil in a non-stick frypan over medium heat. Add garlic chips, white wine and lemon juice.
2. Reduce heat to medium-low. Add oregano, tarragon and basil. Stir.
3. At the same time, cook pasta according to package directions — al dente.
4. When pasta is within 3 minutes of being done, add shrimp to frying pan and cook quickly (3 minutes) on medium to medium-high heat.

Serve hot over cooked pasta and sprinkle with Parmesan cheese.

The crew of the *Molly* and the *Osprey* (both sailboats) combined Shrimp Scampi recipes for this dockside delicacy. They suggest buying shrimp at the local fish market. Clean shrimp by the water spigot on the dock after dusk while enjoying some of the same white wine that is used in the recipe.

Boatswain's Bread

Makes one loaf

Let your guests guess the secret ingredient.

3 cups self-rising flour
3 tablespoons sugar
1 12-ounce can or bottle of beer
⅛ cup plus 1 teaspoon poppy seeds
2 tablespoons butter, melted

1. Preheat oven to 350°.
2. Combine all ingredients, except 1 teaspoon poppy seeds and melted butter.
3. Bake in a 9x5x3-inch greased loaf pan for 55 to 60 minutes until golden.
4. Brush top with melted butter and sprinkle with 1 teaspoon poppy seeds.
5. Remove from pan and cool on rack.

Serve warm with any seafood dish.

Drop Biscuits

Complements any soup on land or sea.

2 cups flour
3 tablespoons baking powder
1 teaspoon salt
¼ cup (½ stick) butter
1 cup milk.

For a change of flavor add ½ cup shredded cheddar cheese after you cut in the butter.

Makes 10 to 12 biscuits

1. Preheat oven to 450°.
2. In a large bowl combine flour, baking powder and salt.
3. Cut in butter until mixture resembles course crumbs.
4. Stir in milk to make a soft dough.
5. Drop dough by large spoonfuls onto a greased cookie sheet or into greased medium size muffin cups.
6. Bake 10 to 12 minutes until lightly browned.

Serve hot!

Breezy Lemon Fluff

Crust:
1 cup flour
½ cup (1 stick) butter
2 tablespoons sugar

Filling:
2 3-ounce packages lemon pie filling
2½ cups sugar
4 egg yolks, beaten
4½ cups water
4 egg whites
1 cup heavy cream, whipped

Serves 12

1. Preheat oven to 375°.
2. Blend flour, butter and 2 tablespoons sugar. Press into a 13x9-inch pan for crust.
3. Bake for 12 to 15 minutes. Cool in pan on wire rack, then refrigerate.

Filling preparation:

1. In a saucepan combine lemon pie filling, 2 cups of the sugar, beaten egg yolks and 2¼ cups of the water. Stir over medium heat.
2. Add the additional 2¼ cups water, stirring briskly. Cook until mixture thickens and begins to boil. Remove from heat and set aside to cool.
3. In mixing bowl beat egg whites until stiff. Add remaining ½ cup sugar. Fold into cooled lemon mixture.
4. Remove crust from refrigerator. Pour in lemon filling and return to refrigerator.
5. Frost with a thin layer of whipped cream before serving.

Ginger Cookies

Makes 60 2-inch round cookies

This cookie gives quick energy while the ginger seems to have a quieting effect on queezy stomachs.

1½ cups sugar
¾ cup (1½ sticks) butter
1 egg
¼ cup molasses
2 cups flour
½ teaspoon salt
1 teaspoon baking soda
1 teaspoon cinnamon
1 teaspoon cloves
1 teaspoon ginger

1. Preheat oven to 375°.
2. Reserve ½ cup sugar in a small bowl.
3. In large bowl cream together 1 cup sugar and butter.
4. Add egg, molasses, flour, salt, baking soda and spices. Mix well and chill 1 hour (dough should be firm.)
5. Form into 1-inch balls and roll in granulated sugar.
6. Place on a greased cookie sheet and bake 8 to 10 minutes.
7. Remove cookies to wire rack to cool.

Upside Down Rhubarb Cake

Makes 16 2-inch squares

Filling:
2 tablespoons butter
¼ cup sugar
¼ cup brown sugar
2¾ cups rhubarb cut in ½-inch pieces

Batter:
⅓ cup butter
⅓ cup sugar
1 egg
½ teaspoon vanilla
1 cup flour
1½ teaspoons baking powder
½ cup milk
rind of 1 orange, grated

Filling preparation:
1. Preheat oven to 350°.
2. Melt butter in 8x8x2-inch pan.
3. Stir in sugars and rhubarb. Spread evenly over bottom of pan and set aside.

Batter preparation:
1. In a mixing bowl cream together butter and sugar.
2. Add egg and vanilla. Beat well.
3. Combine flour and baking powder and add to batter alternating with milk.
4. Stir in orange rind.
5. Pour batter over rhubarb mixture already in pan.
6. Bake for 45 to 55 minutes.
7. Cool 10 minutes before inverting on platter.
8. Serve warm with whipped cream.

Chocolate, Chocolate, Chocolate Mocha Decadence   Serves 10 to 12

Elegant but uncomplicated.

1 package dark chocolate cake mix,
   baked as directed and cooled
1 cup Kahlúa liqueur
3 4-ounce packages dark chocolate instant
   pudding, made as directed
1 16-ounce container prepared
   whipped topping
6 Heath Bars, crushed

**Make 4 layers in large glass bowl
or trifle bowl as follows:**

1. Break up one-quarter of the cake into
   pieces and place in bottom of bowl.
2. Sprinkle ¼ cup of Kahlúa over the cake.
3. Pour one-quarter of the pudding over the
   cake and spread over pieces to cover.
4. Cover that layer with one-quarter of the
   prepared whipped topping.
5. Sprinkle with one-quarter of the broken
   Heath Bars.
6. Repeat process until you have 4 layers
   or run out of room in the bowl,
   whichever comes first.

Port and Starboard Sipper   Makes 4 1-cup servings

This red and green drink will start you on the right course!

1 teaspoon instant chicken bouillon
   granules
1 cup boiling water
3 cups tomato juice
2 tablespoons lime juice
1 teaspoon sugar
1 teaspoon Worcestershire sauce
¼ teaspoon celery salt
¼ teaspoon dried basil, crushed
4 stalks celery with leaves

1. Dissolve bouillon in boiling water.
2. In a pitcher combine dissolved bouillon,
   tomato juice, lime juice, sugar, Worcestershire sauce, celery salt and basil.
3. Cover and chill.
4. To serve, pour into glasses.
5. Garnish each serving with a stalk of celery.

PLAYGROUND PICNIC

SAMPLE MENU

Porcupines

Bunny Hop Soup

Hop Scotch Muffins

Merry Go Round Apples

Iddy Biddy Jello Molds

Best Friend Brownies

Pint-sized pleasures abound at the playground when youngsters gather to enjoy fresh air and free-spirited frolicking. No sound is as sweet as the laughter of children, and it rings out freely in this happy setting. For such outings, experiment with colorful, giddy goodies high in youthful appeal. The following recipes suggest ideas that will delight and excite the "see-saw" set while providing nutrition as well.

Apple-Date Spread

Makes 3 cups

1 8-ounce package cream cheese, softened
¼ cup milk
1½ cups pecans, finely chopped
1 cup unpeeled apple, finely chopped
¾ cup dates, finely chopped
apple slices for garnish
assorted crackers

1. In a bowl, beat together cream cheese and milk.
2. Stir in chopped pecans, apple and dates.
3. Garnish with apple slices and serve with assorted crackers.

Cheesy Fruit And Nut Spread

Makes 1½ cups

3 tablespoons honey
1 tablespoon orange juice
1 8-ounce package cream cheese, softened
½ cup dried apple chunks
¼ cup toasted pecans, chopped
apples
pears
crackers

1. In a bowl, beat honey and orange juice with cream cheese.
2. Stir in dried apple chunks and chopped pecans.
3. Serve with apples, pears and crackers.

Porcupines

Appealing to a child's palate.

Makes 30

1 pound ground beef
½ cup rice, uncooked
2 tablespoons onion, minced
¼ teaspoon chili powder
1 teaspoon salt
½ teaspoon Worcestershire sauce
¼ cup celery, chopped
2 cups tomato juice

1. Preheat oven to 350°.
2. Mix beef, rice, onion, chili powder, salt, Worcestershire sauce and celery.
3. Shape into 1-inch balls.
4. Place in casserole dish.
5. Pour tomato juice over meatballs.
6. Cover and bake 1 hour.

To serve: spoon Porcupines right from the casserole dish.

Sweet Banana Circles

Makes 20

Just right for little fingers.

¼ cup plain yogurt
½ teaspoon almond extract
1 cup walnuts (OR almonds or pecans),
  ground
½ pound unsweetened coconut, shredded
2 ripe bananas

1. In a small mixing bowl, blend together yogurt and almond extract. Set aside.

2. Place nuts and coconut in separate bowls for dipping. Set aside.

3. Peel bananas and cut into rounds ¼-inch thick.

4. One at a time, dip banana slices into yogurt. Then roll them in either nuts or coconut.

5. Place coated bananas in a single layer on jellyroll pan. Freeze for at least 10 minutes before serving.

Can be frozen if not eaten immediately. Freeze on a tray, *uncovered* (1 hour). Transfer to a plastic freezer bag to store.

Bunny Hop Soup

Serves 4

Kids will love this soup served in a mug.

3 cups chicken soup
1 small onion, chopped
4 large carrots, peeled and sliced
⅛ teaspoon nutmeg
2 tablespoons peanut butter
1 tablespoon Worcestershire sauce
1 clove garlic, crushed
dash of Tabasco sauce (optional)
peanuts, chopped
apples, chopped

1. Place all ingredients in a 2- to 3-quart saucepan and simmer until carrots are tender, 20 to 30 minutes. Allow to cool.

2. Place cooked soup in food processor or blender and purée.

3. Return to saucepan and reheat before serving.

4. Can be garnished with chopped peanuts or apples.

Soup is also good served at room temperature.

Florida Baked Beans

Serves 10 to 12

Kids' favorite with hot dogs and hamburgers.

3 strips of bacon, cut into small pieces
1 cup green pepper, chopped
1 cup onion, chopped
1 large (3 pounds, 7 ounces) can
   pork and beans
¼ cup ketchup
½ cup dark brown sugar
1 teaspoon cinnamon
¼ cup prepared mustard
¼ cup molasses

1. In a small frypan cook bacon until crisp.
2. Add peppers and onions and cook until tender. Set aside.
3. In a large bowl mix beans, ketchup, sugar, cinnamon, mustard and molasses.
4. Pour entire mixture into crock pot or oven-proof casserole dish. Add cooked bacon, peppers and onions.
5. Simmer on low in crock pot or in 300° oven for 1 hour.

Hop Scotch Muffins

Makes 12 muffins

A complete meal when served with soup.

2 cups flour
1 tablespoon baking powder
¾ teaspoon salt
¼ teaspoon dry mustard
2 tablespoons sugar
1 egg, beaten
⅓ cup butter, melted
1 cup milk
¾ cup ham, chopped
¾ cup cheddar cheese, grated

1. Preheat oven to 400°.
2. In a large bowl sift together flour, baking powder, salt, mustard and sugar.
3. Stir in egg, butter and milk just until blended.
4. Fold in ham and cheese.
5. Fill paper-lined cups in muffin tin and bake 20 minutes until golden.

Serve hot or cold.

Peanut Butter-Peanut Butter Chip Cookies   Makes 4 dozen

2½ cups flour
1 cup sugar
1 cup brown sugar
½ teaspoon baking soda
½ teaspoon baking powder
1 cup (2 sticks) butter
1 cup peanut butter
2 eggs
2 teaspoons vanilla
1 10-ounce bag peanut butter chips

1. Preheat oven to 375°.
2. In a small bowl combine flour, sugars, baking soda and baking powder.
3. In a separate bowl beat together butter, peanut butter, eggs and vanilla.
4. Slowly add dry ingredients to wet ingredients and mix well at medium speed.
5. Stir in peanut butter chips. (Chocolate chips may be added if desired.)
6. Drop by rounded tablespoonfuls onto an ungreased cookie sheet. OR form dough into 1-inch balls. Place on cookie sheet 2 inches apart. Flatten with a fork.
7. Bake for 10 to 12 minutes.
8. Remove to wire rack to cool.

Peanut Butter Bites   Makes 3 dozen

Who says nourishment has to be boring?

2 cups quick-cooking oats
1 cup whole wheat flour
½ teaspoon baking powder
½ teaspoon baking soda
⅛ teaspoon salt
1 cup smooth peanut butter
1 cup (2 sticks) butter
⅓ cup sugar
⅓ cup light brown sugar
2 eggs
1 teaspoon vanilla
½ cup unsalted peanuts, chopped
⅓ cup spreadable strawberry fruit

1. Preheat oven to 325°.
2. In medium bowl, combine 1⅔ cups oats (reserve ⅓ cup), flour, baking powder, baking soda and salt. Set aside.
3. In a large bowl with mixer at low speed, beat peanut butter and butter. Add sugars, increase speed to high. Beat until light and fluffy.
4. Beat in eggs and vanilla.
5. Stir in oat mixture until well-blended. Add peanuts.
6. Shape dough into 1 inch balls. Roll each in reserved ⅓ cup oats.
7. Place 2 inches apart on ungreased cookie sheet. Press finger into center of each ball to indent.
8. Bake 15 minutes or until browned. Remove cookies to wire rack; cool slightly.
9. Fill cookies with spreadable strawberry fruit.

Best Friend Brownies

Share this recipe with someone you love.

Makes 16 2-inch squares

½ cup (1 stick) butter, softened
⅔ cup sugar
1 teaspoon vanilla
2 large eggs
2 1-ounce packets pre-melted
   unsweetened chocolate
½ cup flour
½ cup walnuts, chopped
2 tablespoons confectioner's sugar

1. Preheat oven to 350°.
2. Cream butter, sugar and vanilla
   in a mixing bowl.
3. Beat in eggs.
4. Blend in chocolate.
5. Stir in flour and nuts.
6. Pour into greased 8-inch square pan.
7. Bake for 25 minutes.
8. Cool on wire rack.
9. When completely cool, top
   with confectioner's sugar.

Iddy Biddy Jello Molds

An excellent idea for picnics.

Serves 4

1 4-ounce package
   lemon flavored gelatin
1 cup boiling water
1 cup cold water
½ cup fruit cocktail, well drained

Also needed for serving:

4 disposable cups
aluminum foil
transparent tape
4 plastic spoons

1. In a large bowl, pour boiling water over
   gelatin. Stir until gelatin is dissolved.
   Add cold water and stir.
2. Place 1 tablespoon of fruit cocktail
   at bottom of each individual cup.
3. Pour gelatin evenly into four cups.
4. Cover each cup with a piece of aluminum
   foil. Tape securely in place. Refrigerate
   3 hours or overnight.
5. Tape plastic spoon to each cup before
   packing in ice filled thermal container.

Merry-Go-Round Apples

Delicious *and* nutritious!

Serves 4

4 apples
½ cup chunky peanut butter

1. Carve out core of apples.
2. Stuff holes with peanut butter.
3. Wrap in plastic wrap or wax paper until ready to serve.

Five Minute Fudge

Makes about 2 pounds

2 tablespoons butter
⅔ cup evaporated milk
1⅔ cups sugar
½ teaspoon salt
2 cups miniature marshmallows
1½ cups chocolate chips
1 teaspoon vanilla

1. Combine butter, milk, sugar and salt in 3-quart saucepan.
2. Bring to a boil, stirring constantly.
3. Boil for 4 to 5 minutes while continuing to stir.
4. Remove from heat.
5. Stir in marshmallows, chocolate chips and vanilla until melted.
6. Pour into greased 8-inch square pan.
7. Cool and cut into squares.

Cowboy Cookies

Head 'em up and move 'em out.

Makes 3 dozen

1 cup (2 sticks) butter
1 cup sugar
1 cup brown sugar
2 eggs
2 cups flour, sifted
1 teaspoon baking soda
½ teaspoon baking powder
½ teaspoon salt
2 cups rolled oats
1 teaspoon vanilla
1 12-ounce package chocolate chips

1. Preheat oven to 350°.
2. Cream together butter and sugars.
3. Beat in eggs.
4. Stir in dry ingredients.
5. Add vanilla and chocolate chips. Mix well.
6. Drop by rounded tablespoons on ungreased cookie sheet.
7. Bake for 15 minutes.
8. Remove cookies to wire rack to cool.

SABINO CRUISE

SAMPLE MENU

Overboard Punch

Shrimply Divine Mousse

Mystic Clam Chowder

Quiche Cargo Boat

Fruit Splash

Gingerbread Buoys

The Mystic River drawbridge in charming, downtown Mystic opens to allow the double-decked *Sabino* to pass on summer evenings. Mystic Seaport's coal-fired, steam-driven vessel is, like the drawbridge, a well-known local attraction. The scenic down-river voyage, which unfailingly enthralls passengers, can be further enhanced when mouth-watering provisions are stowed aboard. Sample some of the following mystical masterpieces that make the passage even more pleasurable.

Shrimply Divine Mousse

Serves 12

1 8-ounce can tomato soup, undiluted
1 8-ounce package cream cheese, softened
1 cup mayonnaise
1½ envelopes unflavored gelatin
¼ cup cold water
1 pound frozen small shrimp,
  thawed and drained
½ cup scallions, diced
½ cup celery, diced
1 tablespoon horseradish

1. In a saucepan over low heat stir soup and cream cheese until smooth and creamy.
2. Remove from heat and stir in mayonnaise until smooth.
3. Dilute gelatin in ¼ cup cold water and add to cream cheese mixture.
4. Stir in shrimp, scallions, celery and horseradish.
5. Pour into greased mold and chill.
6. Invert on serving platter just before serving.

Use a fish-shaped mold and fish-shaped crackers for a festive presentation.

Florentine Pasta Salad

Serves 4 to 6

1 9-ounce package fresh linquine
  or fettuccine
½ cup Pesto Sauce
  (see index for recipe)
2 tablespoons lemon juice
2 cups fresh spinach, shredded
1 cup tomato, coarsely chopped
¾ cup red onion, thinly sliced
¼ cup toasted pine nuts
¼ cup Parmesan cheese, grated

1. Cook linguine according to package directions. Drain and cool under cold running water; drain thoroughly.
2. In large mixing bowl, combine Pesto Sauce and lemon juice.
3. Add linguine; toss gently.
4. Add spinach, tomato, onion and toss until coated.
5. Spoon onto individual plates or large platter.
6. Sprinkle with pine nuts.
7. Top with Parmesan.

Pepper Salad

Serves 8

2 green peppers
2 red peppers
2 yellow peppers
2 tablespoons olive oil
½ teaspoon thyme
¼ teaspoon salt
¼ teaspoon pepper
2 cups jicama strips
  or water chestnuts

1. Seed peppers and cut into ¼-inch strips.
2. In a small saucepan, sauté peppers in oil about 5 minutes. (They should be tender, but crisp.)
3. Stir in seasonings, except for jicama.
4. Stir in the jicama just before serving.

Grammy Geltz's Cucumbers

Serves 4

A treasure from the family recipe chest.

3 large cucumbers
salt
1 8-ounce container sour cream
2 cloves garlic, crushed
¼ teaspoon dill
¼ teaspoon pepper

Variation: Omit the garlic and substite 2 tablespoons very finely chopped onion.

1. Peel and slice cucumbers paper thin. Sprinkle generously with salt. Place cucumbers in colander and press using weighted plate for 2 to 3 hours allowing liquid to drain away.
2. In a large bowl mix together sour cream, garlic, dill and pepper. Refrigerate.
3. When cucumbers are well drained, squeeze as much remaining juice from them as possible using hands.
4. Add cucumbers to sour cream mixture. Chill thoroughly before serving.

Woodland Mushroom Soup

Serves 6 to 8

1 ounce dried cepes or poricini mushrooms
1 cup water
½ cup (1 stick) butter
1 cup onions, minced
2 pounds fresh mushrooms, sliced
1½ quarts (6 cups) chicken stock
2 teaspoons salt
¼ teaspoon pepper
2 cups heavy cream

Variations: Add 6 tablespoons Madeira to stock. No dried mushrooms? Extrude liquid from sliced mushrooms in 400° oven for 10 minutes. Put extruded liquid in pot and reduce by half. When adding stock, add extruded liquid as well.

1. Soak dried mushrooms in 1 cup water and set aside.
2. Melt butter in large stockpot. Add onions, cover and cook for 15 minutes until soft but not brown.
3. Add sliced fresh mushrooms and cook for 10 minutes, stirring occasionally.
4. Rinse the dried mushrooms and add to stockpot along with chicken stock, salt and pepper. Cook for 15 minutes. Cool slightly.
5. Pour into blender container and purée until smooth.
6. Return to pot, add cream and stir until blended.

Serve hot.

135

Mystic Clam Chowder

Serves 16

Yes, you <u>do</u> grind clams, potatoes and onions.

1 quart clams
6 medium potatoes
4 medium onions
1 quart clam juice
4 tablespoons butter
½ teaspoon salt
¼ teaspoon pepper
⅛ teaspoon thyme
¼ teaspoon parsley flakes
¼ teaspoon onion powder
1½ quarts light cream

1. Into a large stockpot, grind clams, potatoes and onions.

2. Add clam juice, butter and herbs.

3. Simmer covered, 30 minutes.

4. Warm light cream. Add to chowder ingredients and stir.

Can be frozen by pint portions before adding cream.

Quiche Cargo Boat

Serves 8 to 10

This luscious "boat" will please every crewmember

1 loaf french bread, unsliced
2 tablespoons butter
½ cup scallions, chopped
1½ teaspoons flour
1 cup Swiss or cheddar cheese, shredded
½ cup light cream
2 teaspoons cornstarch
2 eggs, lightly beaten
¼ teaspoon dry mustard
¼ teaspoon salt
¼ teaspoon pepper
1 tablespoon Parmesan cheese, grated

Variations: Crumbled bacon, ham, basil, mushrooms, cooked shrimp, broccoli or spinach may be added to the egg mixture.

1. Preheat oven to 425°.

2. Cut off top of bread and hollow out, leaving about 1-inch of bread on bottom. Cover with foil. Place on baking sheet and bake 5 minutes.

3. While bread is in oven, melt butter in saucepan and sauté scallions until tender. Mix in flour and set aside.

4. Layer shredded cheese and any cooked meats or vegetables you might want to add in the bottom of the bread shell.

5. In a medium bowl stir small amount of the cream into cornstarch, blending until smooth.

6. Add remaining cream, eggs and seasonings. Mix well and add to the onion mixture.

7. Pour cream mixture over cheese in bread shell.

8. Sprinkle with Parmesan. Bake 40 minutes or until inserted knife comes out clean.

9. Let stand 10 minutes before slicing. Serve or wrap to go.

Shooter's Sandwich

Serves 6

Your hunter will love it, tradition and all.

1½ pound loaf day old white bread,
   unsliced OR seeded rye bread, unsliced
¼ cup (½ stick) butter
½ teaspoon thyme
½ teaspoon oregano
1 tablespoon parsley, minced
1¼ pound ground round
1 teaspoon salt
½ teaspoon pepper
2 tablespoons scallions, chopped
1 teaspoon mustard
1 tablespoon Worcestershire sauce
1 tablespoon tomato paste
½ teaspoon curry powder
1 egg, beaten
2 tablespoons milk

1. Preheat oven to 350°.
2. Cut a 1-inch thick slice from one end of the loaf. Scoop out the inside of the bread, leaving a ¾-inch thick crust at top, bottom and sides.
3. In a small saucepan melt butter and combine with thyme, oregano and parsley. Brush inside of loaf and end piece with butter mixture.
4. Make breadcrumbs from inside of loaf. In a large bowl combine ½ cup of crumbs with ground round, salt, pepper, scallions, mustard, Worcestershire sauce, tomato paste, curry powder and beaten egg.
5. Pack meat mixture into hollow loaf.
6. Replace sliced and buttered end and tie in place. Brush with milk.
7. Wrap loaf loosely in greased foil. Bake for 1½ hours.
8. Let loaf cool to room temperature or wrap in newspaper to keep warm.

Remember to pack sharp knife.

This is a customary picnic choice of the "guns" (hunters) in Scotland and England. It has been said "With this shooter's sandwich and a flask of whiskey-and-water, a man may travel from Land's End to John O'Grouts and snap his fingers at both." No wonder! It's made with a whole loaf of bread scooped out and filled with ground meat and herbs.

137

Vegetable Pizza

Serves 4 to 6

Banish the vegetable platter and dip.

2 tubes refrigerated crescent rolls
2 3-ounce packages cream cheese
⅓ cup mayonnaise
½ (1.1-ounce) package dry original
   ranch dressing

Suggested raw chopped vegetables:

parsley
mushrooms
carrots
broccoli
onion
zucchini
red or green pepper
radish

Requires some advance preparation.

1. Remove rolls from container and pat flat in 11x7-inch pan.
2. Bake according to package directions. Cool.
3. Mix together cream cheese, mayonnaise and dressing mix. Spread over cooled crust.
4. Sprinkle top with parsley and a combination of raw vegetables.
5. Cover and refrigerate 6 to 8 hours before serving.

To keep vegetables from discoloring, cover tightly with plastic wrap.

Vegetable Casserole

Serves 10 to 12

Sure to bring rave reviews. Even landlubbers will yell, Ahoy!

1 package frozen green beans, thawed
1 can white shoe peg corn, drained
1 can cream of celery soup
½ cup sour cream
½ cup sharp cheddar cheese, grated
½ cup celery, chopped
½ cup onion, chopped
½ cup green pepper, chopped
½ teaspoon salt
½ teaspoon pepper

Topping:
½ cup (1 stick) butter
½ large box buttery crackers, crumbled
½ cup slivered almonds

1. Preheat oven to 350°.
2. Combine beans and corn in a large bowl.
3. Add remaining ingredients and blend well.
4. In a fry pan, melt butter for topping. Stir in cracker crumbs and almonds. Sprinkle on top of the casserole, cover and bake for 40 minutes.
5. Remove cover for last 5 minutes or until top is browned.

Fruit Splash

Serves 8 to 10

Dive into this at breakfast, too.

5 cups assorted melon balls
1 8-ounce carton lemon yogurt
1 tablespoon orange juice
2 ounces whipped dessert topping, thawed
3 medium apples, cored and chopped
½ cup broken pecans

1. Chill melon balls in tight container until serving time.
2. Stir together yogurt and juice. Fold in dessert topping. Stir in apples, cover and chill.
3. To serve, spoon apple mixture in glass bowl. Sprinkle with pecans.
4. Spoon melon balls over apple mixture. Let apples show around edges.

Orange Bread Pudding

Serves 6

4 eggs
2 cups lowfat milk
3 tablespoons fructose
½ teaspoon orange rind, grated
¼ teaspoon cinnamon
1 teaspoon vanilla
6 slices whole wheat bread,
  cut into cubes
1 tablespoon raisins
orange juice, frozen concentrate,
  thawed

Freeze end pieces or crusts from an assortment of breads to use for bread pudding.

1. Preheat oven to 300°.
2. In a large mixing bowl beat eggs until fluffy.
3. Add milk and fructose to eggs. Mix well.
4. Stir in orange rind, cinnamon and vanilla.
5. Add bread cubes to liquid.
6. Pour into 8-inch square baking dish.
7. Sprinkle with raisins.
8. Place baking pan in larger pan filled with 2 inches of water.
9. Bake for 30 minutes.
10. Remove pan from water, brush pudding with undiluted orange juice, and cool on wire rack.

Serve warm or cold.

Graham Pudding

Serves 8 to 10

Consistency of moist cake. Texture improves with time.

11 whole 2½x4½-inch graham crackers, ground
2 cups sugar
1 cup walnuts, ground
1 teaspoon baking powder
5 egg yolks, beaten
5 egg whites, beaten until stiff

1. Preheat oven to 400°.
2. Mix all dry ingredients in a large bowl.
3. Add beaten egg yolks and mix well until mixture is consistency of sand.
4. Fold in stiffly beaten egg whites.
5. Pour into a 9-inch pie pan and bake for 15 to 20 minutes until toothpick inserted in center of pudding comes out clean.
6. Cool in pan. Serve with whipped cream or ice cream.

In the 1950s this pudding was made and sent weekly via Air Mail to a family member serving with the American Red Cross in Korea. This was a "look forward to treat."

Overboard Punch

Makes 25 8-ounce servings

Sip slowly and try to stay on an even keel.

1 12-ounce can frozen orange juice, thawed
1 12-ounce can frozen lemonade, thawed
1 6-ounce can frozen daiquiri mix, thawed
1 6-ounce can frozen pineapple juice, thawed
2 quarts cold water
3 quarts ginger ale
1 ice ring
orange slices
a few sprigs of mint

1. In a large container combine orange juice, lemonade, daiquiri mix, pineapple juice, water and ginger ale.
2. Pour into a punch bowl over an ice ring.
3. Decorate top of punch with orange slices and mint.

The daiquiri mix may be eliminated.
Hint: Make the ice ring with fruit juice.

Gingerbread Buoys

Summer or winter — always a favorite.

Makes 3 dozen

⅓ cup light brown sugar, firmly packed
⅓ cup light molasses
¾ teaspoon ginger
¼ teaspoon cinnamon
¼ teaspoon cloves
2¼ teaspoons baking soda
⅓ cup butter
I egg
2½ cups flour

1. Combine sugar, molasses, ginger, cinnamon and cloves in large saucepan. Bring to a boil. Remove from heat.
2. Add baking soda and butter, stirring until mixture thickens and butter melts.
3. Add egg and beat vigorously. Stir in 2¼ cups flour.
4. Spread remaining cups flour on wooden board, place dough on top. Knead until flour is well combined and dough is smooth.
5. Shape into a ball. Wrap in plastic wrap. Refrigerate 1½ hours until firm.
6. Cut dough into quarters. Roll each about ⅛-inch thick, between 2 sheets of wax paper. Refrigerate until thoroughly chilled, for easier handling.
7. Preheat oven to 350°. Lightly grease cookie sheets.
8. Cut dough into desired shapes. Using spatula, place I inch apart on prepared cookie sheets.
9. Bake 5 to 6 minutes. Remove cookies to wire rack to cool.

Fresh Fruit Spritzers

Makes 6 8-ounce servings

2 fresh peaches, peeled and sliced
6 fresh cherries with stems
½ cup cherry brandy
¼ cup peach brandy
2 teaspoons ascorbic acid color keeper*
I 750ml bottle Moselle wine, chilled
2 cups carbonated soda water, chilled

*Ascorbic acid can be found in the canning section of the supermarket.

1. In a large pitcher, mix peaches, cherries, brandies and ascorbic acid color keeper.
2. Refrigerate 8 hours or overnight. Chill 6 stemmed glasses.
3. At serving time, add wine and carbonated soda water to mixture in pitcher. Stir gently.
4. Serve in chilled glasses, garnished with peach slices and cherries.

HIKING · CYCLING · CAMPING

SAMPLE MENU

Bug Juice

Smoked Eggstacy

Piggy Back Satay With Peanut Sauce

Tentalizing Sunset Salad

Flat Tire Bread

10K Ginger Snaps

Bug Bites

Minted Canteen Brew

Glorious sunrises and sunsets, the scents of pine, wildflowers or salt air and the vistas of mountains, meadows or sandy beaches all contribute to the pleasures of hiking, cycling and camping. Food for backpackers should be as inspiring as the settings they encounter and energizing enough to allow them to pursue yet one more turn in the road. In this section we've included recipes that travel well. The only problem is you will want to try all of them, and that could mean a very weighty walk.

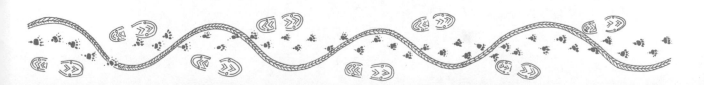

Smoked Eggstacy

Serves 6

6 eggs
2 tablespoons salt
¼ cup soy sauce
2 whole star anise
2 tablespoons smokey loose tea
  (Hu-Kwa or Earl Grey)

1. In medium saucepan, place eggs and cover with water. Bring water to a boil over high heat. Lower heat and simmer 10 minutes. Cover pan and remove from heat. Let eggs cool in water.

2. When cool, drain water.

3. Tap the egg shells lightly all over with the back of a spoon until all the shells are completely cracked.

4. Return eggs to pan and cover with cold water.

5. Add salt, soy sauce, anise and tea. Bring to a boil, reduce heat and simmer very slowly 2 to 3 hours, stirring occasionally. Remove pan from heat and let eggs sit in the liquid for 8 hours.

6. Drain eggs and refrigerate in shells, until ready to serve. Foil-wrapped, eggs will keep for 1 week.

7. Serve, peeled and halved, with Sesame Salt.

Sesame Salt:

¼ cup sesame seeds
½ cup coarse salt
1 teaspoon fresh pepper

Requires advance preparation.

Sesame Salt preparation:

1. Lightly toast sesame seeds in hot ungreased frypan over high heat, stirring constantly.

2. Mix toasted sesame seeds with salt and pepper. Place in shaker until ready to serve.

Tentalizing Sunset Salad

Serves 6 to 8

1 head broccoli, cut into florets
2 carrots, sliced diagonally
2 tablespoons water
1 small red pepper, cut in strips
1 small yellow pepper, cut in strips
1 8-ounce can water chestnuts, drained and sliced
2 scallions, sliced diagonally
1 14-ounce can whole baby corn, drained

1. Combine broccoli and carrots with 2 tablespoons water in a microwaveable container with lid and cook on high for 4 minutes. Drain well and cool.

2. Place cooled broccoli and carrots in plastic bag with remaining vegetables. Set aside.

Dressing:

3 tablespoons peanut oil
3 tablespoons rice wine vinegar
2 tablespoons soy sauce
1 teaspoon ginger root, grated
1 teaspoon sesame oil
½ teaspoon crushed red pepper
1 clove garlic, crushed
¼ cup toasted sesame seeds

Dressing preparation:

1. Mix together all dressing ingredients and pour over vegetables in plastic bag. Seal bag and toss vegetables, coating all with dressing.

2. Before refrigerating, squeeze air out of bag and seal. This will hold for 48 hours, and will travel well.

Best Fajitas

¡Ay, que bueno!

Serves 4 to 6

1 pound boneless skinless chicken breasts
3 tablespoons olive oil
3 tablespoons lime juice, freshly squeezed
3 tablespoons Tequila
3 cloves garlic, crushed
1 to 2 small hot jalapeño peppers, minced
1 package 8 inch flour tortillas
1 green pepper, sliced and grilled
1 onion, sliced and grilled
½ cup sour cream

1. Wash chicken breasts and pat dry. Place chicken in large shallow dish.

2. Combine oil, lime juice, tequila, garlic and jalapeño peppers. Stir and pour over chicken.

3. Cover dish with plastic wrap, place in refrigerator, and marinate overnight, or at least six hours.

4. Remove chicken, discard marinade and grill over hot coals, 3 to 4 minutes per side or until done. (Broil as an alternative.)

5. Slice lengthwise and serve in warm tortillas, adding grilled green pepper, onion, sour cream and Guacamole.

Leftovers are delicious cold, alone or in a sandwich.

Guacamole:

1 ripe avocado
1 tablespoon lemon juice
2 tablespoons onion, grated
½ teaspoon jalapeño pepper, minced
1 clove garlic, crushed
1 tablespoon fresh cilantro (coriander), chopped
½ cup fresh tomato, peeled, seeded and chopped

Guacamole preparation: Makes 1 cup

1. In a medium bowl, mash avocado.

2. Add all other ingredients and mix well.

3. Store in plastic container with tight fitting lid.

4. "Burp" lid to allow air to escape.

Guacamole will eventually darken. Eat within 12 hours.

Mustard Chicken

Serves 8 to 10

5 whole boneless chicken breasts
2 cups English muffin crumbs (3 muffins)
⅔ cup Parmesan cheese, grated
¼ cup parsley, chopped
¾ cup (1½ sticks) butter, melted
2 cloves garlic, crushed
2 tablespoons Dijon mustard
¾ teaspoon Worcestershire sauce

Can be taken along frozen for the first evening meal.

1. Preheat oven to 350°.
2. Cut chicken breasts in half.
3. Mix muffin crumbs, Parmesan cheese and parsley in a pie plate. Set aside.
4. In a large frypan melt butter. Add garlic, mustard and Worcestershire sauce. Keep warm.
5. Dip each chicken breast in butter mixture, then in crumb mixture.
6. Place each chicken breast in a greased 9x13-inch baking dish.
7. Sprinkle any remaining butter and crumb mixture over chicken breasts.
8. Cover with foil and bake for 30 to 40 minutes.
9. Increase oven temperature to 400°. Remove foil and continue baking until browned.

To Freeze: after cooling, wrap each chicken breast in foil and place in freezer.

To Reheat: open foil and place in a 350° oven for approximately 30 minutes or until thoroughly heated.

Baby Ham And Cheese Sandwiches   Serves 10 to 12

½ cup (1 stick) butter, softened
½ teaspoon poppy seeds
1 teaspoon Worcestershire sauce
1 teaspoon Dijon mustard
½ small onion, minced
20 small dinner rolls
½ pound shaved ham
¼ pound Swiss cheese, thinly sliced

Can be made ahead and frozen.

1. Preheat oven to 350°.
2. Combine butter, poppy seeds, Worcestershire sauce, mustard and onion.
3. Spread mixture onto split rolls.
4. Place ham on bottom of rolls, top with cheese and close sandwich with tops of rolls.
5. Place the filled rolls in a foil pan and cover with foil.
6. Bake 15 minutes.

Serve right from pan.
Will remain warm wrapped in foil.

Piggy Back Satay With Peanut Sauce   Serves 4 to 6

And you thought you could only grill hot dogs and hamburgers at a campsite!

1½ pound boneless pork loin OR
   boneless country ribs OR chicken
8" bamboo skewers, soaked in water
   24 hours to prevent burning

Marinade:

¼ cup soy sauce
¼ cup dry sherry
3 tablespoons peanut oil
1 tablespoon brown sugar
2 tablespoons ginger root, grated
2 cloves garlic, crushed

Peanut Sauce:

2 tablespoons chunky peanut butter
1 tablespoon Sake
2 teaspoons hot & spicy oil (Szechuan style)
2 teaspoons sesame oil
2 tablespoons soy sauce
2 teaspoons Worcestershire sauce
1 teaspoon lemon juice
2 tablespoons garlic, crushed
1 tablespoon ginger, minced
2 teaspoons sugar

Requires some advance preparation.

Meat and Marinade preparation:

1. Partially freeze meat (approximately 30 minutes) to facilitate slicing. Cut into thin 1x5-inch strips.
2. Combine all marinade ingredients in a baking dish.
3. Place pork strips in marinade being sure meat is entirely covered.
4. Cover and refrigerate overnight.
5. When ready to travel remove meat from refrigerator.
6. Skewer meat with bamboo skewers and place in large self-locking plastic bag or plastic rectangular containers with tight-fitting lid.
7. Pour in marinade and you're ready to take your barbecue on the road.
8. When ready to cook: Grill meat 5 minutes on each side.
9. Remove meat from skewer and serve hot with Peanut Sauce.

Peanut Sauce preparation.

1. Mix all ingredients together. Sauce will be thick.
2. Place in container with lid.

Be sure to pack charcoal and matches or better yet, a small portable propane grill.

Brunner Beaners   Serves 4 to 6

2 15-ounce cans red kidney beans
1 medium onion, finely chopped
⅓ cup brown sugar
⅓ cup cider vinegar
1 unpeeled apple, finely chopped

1. Place beans and onion in a large pot. Over high heat, bring to boil. Lower heat, cover and simmer 20 minutes.
2. Add sugar and vinegar. Simmer 20 minutes, uncovered.
3. Add apple. Simmer until juice is thick and apple is done (about 20 minutes).

Vermont Baked Beans

Serves 6 to 8

This was once served every Saturday night with homemade bread and pickles as accompaniments.

1 pound dry Navy or pea beans
½ teaspoon baking soda
½ pound salt pork, sliced
1 large onion
½ cup Vermont maple syrup
1 cup molasses
½ teaspoon dry mustard
½ teaspoon salt
water to cover beans

Requires some advance preparation.

1. Soak beans in cold water overnight.
2. In morning, par boil 10 minutes with baking soda. Drain.
3. Place 3 or 4 slices of salt pork in bottom of bean pot. Add half the beans, onion and more salt pork, reserving 3 slices for the top. Cover with remaining beans and salt pork.
4. Add maple syrup, molasses, mustard and salt. Cover with water.
5. Bake at 275° for 5 to 6 hours.

Serve with Boston Brown Bread (see index) and Jerry's Quick Pickles (see index).

Pepperoni Bread

Makes 2 loaves

Easy but impressive.

2 loaves frozen bread dough
1 green pepper, sliced lengthwise
1 tablespoon oil
⅓ pound pepperoni, sliced
½ pound Provolone cheese, sliced
1 tablespoon Parmesan cheese, grated
½ teaspoon garlic powder

1. Preheat oven to 350°.
2. Line a jellyroll pan with foil and spray with non-stick spray.
3. Thaw dough according to package directions.
4. Fry pepper in 1 tablespoon of oil and cool.
5. Stretch dough to have each loaf measure approximately 6x15-inches.
6. In each loaf layer pepperoni, Provolone and green pepper. Sprinkle with Parmesan cheese and garlic powder.
7. Roll dough jellyroll style. Seal well.
8. Brush top with oil from peppers.
9. Bake 25 minutes until golden brown.
10. Remove and let cool in pan 15 minutes before cutting.

Serve hot or at room temperature.

Flat Tire Bread

Serves 4

Don't let the length of the directions keep you from traveling this culinary road.

¼ cup sesame seeds, toasted
2 cups flour
¾ cup boiling water
2 tablespoons sesame oil
I teaspoon salt
¼ cup scallions
I tablespoon fresh coriander (cilantro),
   finely minced
¼ cup peanut oil

1. In a small ungreased frypan, over high heat, stir sesame seeds until golden. Set aside to cool.

2. In a medium bowl, mix flour and boiling water. Stir well.

3. Knead dough on lightly floured board, until smooth and elastic (5 minutes). Cover bowl and let dough rest 20 minutes

4. Roll dough on lightly floured board into a square ½-inch thick.

5. With pastry brush, spread top evenly with sesame oil. Sprinkle entire surface with salt, then scallions, coriander and 3 tablespoons toasted sesame seeds.

6. Roll dough tightly in a cylinder, jellyroll style. Pinch edges of dough to seal, then twist dough several times as though you were wringing water from a cloth.

7. Beginning at one end, wind the dough into a flat coil, tucking the end under and toward center of coil.

8. With rolling pin, roll and flatten coil to ½-inch thickness. Sprinkle remaining I tablespoon sesame seeds on both sides of dough.

9. Roll out dough again to a circle ¼-inch thick. (Can be refrigerated at this point if not ready to serve. Place dough between pieces of floured wax paper, cover with plastic wrap and refrigerate.)

10. Place a large frypan over medium heat and when evenly heated, add ¼ cup peanut oil.

11. Add dough and fry on both sides 4 to 5 minutes on each side, until golden brown.

Serve hot or cold.

Boston Brown Bread

Makes 2 loaves

1½ cups whole wheat flour
½ cup white flour, sifted
½ cup corn meal
2 teaspoons baking soda
1 teaspoon salt
1 cup raisins
2 cups buttermilk
½ cup molasses, preferably dark

1. Mix dry ingredients in mixing bowl.
2. Stir in raisins.
3. Combine buttermilk and molasses. Stir into dry ingredients.
4. Spoon batter into 2 greased 1-pound coffee cans and allow to stand for 30 minutes.
5. Preheat oven to 350°.
6. Bake 40 to 50 minutes, until cake tester comes out clean when inserted into bread.
7. Remove bread from cans to cake rack for cooling.

10K Ginger Snaps

You'll keep running back for more.

Makes 4 dozen

1 cup (2 sticks) unsalted butter
2 cups sugar
3 tablespoons fresh ginger, minced
2 eggs, beaten
½ cup molasses
1½ teaspoons white pepper
1½ teaspoons vinegar
1½ teaspoons baking soda
½ teaspoon cinnamon
¼ teaspoon cloves
4 cups flour

1. Cream butter and sugar in a food processor until fluffy.
2. Add ginger, eggs, molasses, pepper and vinegar. Process until combined.
3. Add baking soda, cinnamon, and cloves. Process again to combine.
4. Add flour, 1 cup at a time, until dough forms a ball.
5. Divide dough into four portions. Wrap each with plastic wrap and refrigerate several hours.
6. Preheat oven to 350°.
7. Remove dough from refrigerator and roll each portion on a lightly floured board to ¼-inch thickness.
8. Cut into shapes related to your special event.
9. Place 1 inch apart on a greased cookie sheet and bake 10 to 12 minutes.
10. Cool cookies on wire rack.

Rosalie's Coconut Pound Cake

Serves 10 to 12

1½ cups (3 sticks) butter
3 cups sugar
5 eggs
1 5-ounce can evaporated milk,
  diluted with water to make 1 cup
3 cups flour
dash salt
1 teaspoon vanilla
1 teaspoon almond extract
1 6-ounce can flake coconut

Be sure to use *canned* coconut.

1. Preheat oven to 325°.
2. Cream butter and sugar until creamy.
3. Add eggs one at a time, beating after each addition.
4. Add milk alternately with flour, beating after each addition.
5. Stir in salt, vanilla and almond extract.
6. Fold in coconut and mix thoroughly.
7. Pour into well greased and floured bundt pan or 2 bread pans.
8. Bake 1½ hours.
9. Remove from pan and cool on wire rack.

Bermudian Banana Bread

Makes 1 loaf

This atypical banana bread is very ap"peel"ing.

1½ cups flour
1 teaspoon salt
1 teaspoon baking soda
¾ cup dark brown sugar
⅓ cup butter
2 eggs, beaten
2 small bananas, mashed
⅓ cup milk

1. Preheat oven to 350°.
2. In small bowl sift together flour, salt and baking soda. Set aside.
3. In large bowl cream sugar and butter.
4. Add eggs, one at a time, to butter mixture, mixing well. Add mashed bananas and mix thoroughly.
5. Gradually add dry ingredients, alternating with milk, continuing to mix.
6. Pour into greased 9x5x3-inch loaf pan coated with bread crumbs.
7. Bake for 1 hour.
8. Cool in pan on wire rack for 5 minutes. Remove bread from pan and continue to cool.

Bug Bites

Makes 24 bites

These will keep you nibbling.

1 12-ounce package semi-sweet chocolate
3 tablespoons peanut butter
3 cups chinese noodles or corn flakes

1. In double boiler, melt chocolate and peanut butter.
2. Stir melted mixture into chinese noodles and blend well.
3. Spoon or scoop small portions (1 to 2 tablespoons) onto waxed paper.
4. Allow to cool and harden before removing and storing in container.

Grand Granola

Makes 3 quarts

A mainstay breakfast for the traveler. Serve with yogurt.

6 cups rolled oats
1 cup wheat germ
1 cup coconut, shredded
1 cup sunflower seeds
1 cup walnuts, chopped
1 cup sesame seeds
1 cup sliced almonds
1 cup dry milk powder
1 cup vegetable oil
1 cup honey
2 teaspoons cinnamon
2 teaspoons vanilla

Will keep several weeks.
Freeze for even longer storage.

1. Preheat oven to 200°.
2. In a large bowl or pan, mix oats, wheat germ, coconut, sunflower seeds, walnuts, sesame seeds, almonds and milk powder.
3. Pour oil, honey, cinnamon and vanilla into a small pan and heat, stirring until hot but not boiling.
4. Pour over oat mixture and stir until evenly moistened. Spread mixture on 2 large rimmed 13x9x2-inch baking pans.
5. Bake uncovered for 1 hour, stirring every 15 minutes.
6. Allow to cool thoroughly and then store in airtight containers.

Jerry's Quick Pickles

Makes 2 quarts

10 small pickling cucumbers, sliced
8 cloves garlic, chopped
½ cup Kosher salt
1 teaspoon black pepper
2½ cups sugar
1 quart white vinegar
1 tablespoon dill
1 tablespoon mustard seed

1. Combine all ingredients.
2. Pack sliced cucumbers in clean jars and cover with liquid. Cover with lid and refrigerate.
3. Ready to eat in a week to 10 days.

Good and crunchy indefinitely, if kept cold.

Crispy Rice Treats

Not the usual recipe.

Makes 20 2-inch squares

1½ cups crisp brown rice cereal
1½ cups raisins, chopped
2 cups walnuts, toasted and chopped
1 cup barley malt or rice syrup or honey
¼ cup tahini

1. Lightly oil an 8x11-inch pan.
2. Place cereal, raisins and walnuts in bowl.
3. Heat malt and tahini in small saucepan stirring constantly.
4. When creamy, slowly bring to a boil and simmer 2 to 3 minutes.
5. Pour over cereal and mix thoroughly.
6. Press into pan and let set for 30 minutes before cutting into squares.

Minted Canteen Brew

Garnish with lemon slices and sprigs of mint.

Makes 6 8-ounce servings

1 cup fresh mint leaves
½ cup sugar
4 herbal tea bags, such as
  raspberry, blackberry or red zinger
1 cup water
1 6-ounce can frozen pink grapefruit juice
  concentrate plus 3 cans water
1½ cups seltzer water
lemon slices for garnish
mint sprigs for garnish

1. In medium saucepan combine mint leaves, sugar, tea bags and 1 cup water.
2. Bring to a boil over high heat.
3. Boil until sugar dissolves, about 2 minutes.
4. Reduce heat to low, cover and simmer 10 minutes.
5. Remove from heat and let steep 30 minutes.
6. Place sieve over large pitcher. Strain mint mixture into pitcher. Discard mint and tea bags.
7. Add juice and water to pitcher.
8. Chill at least 1 hour.
9. Add seltzer water to glasses just before serving.
10. Pour into canteens or thermal cooler with ice.

Hint: When serving iced tea, reserve a portion of tea mixture to make ice cubes. Use these ice cubes when serving tea to prevent drink from becoming watery.

TAILGATING

RAH RAH!

SAMPLE MENU

Stacy's Homecoming Hummus Yummus

Siss-Boom-Bah Soup

Pigskin Pies

Victory Salad

Extra Point Peas

Lenore's Team Color Cookies

Coach's Hot Mocha Coffee

Mirthful occasions which cause fans to rally round the hometeam raise everyone's spirits and evoke cheers. For this reason, tailgating is extremely popular. The food served can be as varied as the players themselves, light and quick or heavy and hearty. Anything goes, from paper plates on oilcloth to fine china and linen. By using these recipe "winners", those responsible for providing the fantastic fare are sure to be voted the most valuable members of the tailgating team.

Stacy's Homecoming Hummus Yummus   Makes 4 cups

A real winner no matter where it's served.

4 cloves garlic
1 teaspoon cumin
1 teaspoon salt
¼ teaspoon pepper
2 1-pound cans chick peas,
  drained, reserving ½ cup liquid
1 cup tahini
¼ cup lemon juice
¼ cup olive oil

Requires some advance preparation.

1. With motor running, drop garlic into food processor until minced.
2. Add cumin, salt and pepper and blend.
3. Add chick peas, tahini and ½ cup liquid. Process until smooth.
4. With processor motor running, add lemon juice and olive oil, a little at a time until mixture is smooth.
5. Chill several hours before serving with Pita chips.

Chicken Ham Pinwheels

Serves 10 to 12

6 boneless chicken breast halves
  (about 1½ pounds)
1 tablespoon Dijon mustard
½ teaspoon pepper
¼ teaspoon garlic powder
¼ teaspoon onion salt
6 ham slices, thinly sliced
paprika
25 slices rye party bread
  OR other thin bread cut in quarters
leaf lettuce
2 tomatoes, thinly sliced
1 cucumber, sliced ¼-inch thick
mustard sauce and mayonnaise

1. Preheat oven to 350°.
2. Pound chicken breasts until ¼-inch thick.
3. Spread Dijon mustard thinly on chicken breasts.
4. Combine pepper, garlic powder and onion salt. Sprinkle over mustard.
5. Place ham slice on each breast, folding ham to fit.
6. Starting with long edge, roll up chicken with ham inside. Secure with toothpicks.
7. Place rolls seam-side down in greased baking pan. Sprinkle with paprika.
8. Bake at 350° for 35 minutes until no longer pink. Cool chicken in pan. Refrigerate until ready to serve.

To Serve:

1. Cut chicken rolls in ¼-inch slices.
2. Place mustard and mayonnaise in small serving bowls.
3. Line serving platter with lettuce. Arrange chicken slices down one side, tomatoes and cucumbers in middle, and bread slices on opposite side.

Let everyone serve themselves.

Avocado Mousse

Serves 4

A wonderfully appetizing way to serve avocado.

1 envelope unflavored gelatin
¼ cup water
1 cup sour cream
1 ripe avocado, peeled and mashed
¼ cup scallions, chopped
2 teaspoons lemon juice
⅛ teaspoon Tabasco sauce

1. Soften gelatin in water in a saucepan. Heat slowly and stir until dissolved.
2. Cool.
3. In a bowl combine sour cream, avocado, scallions, lemon juice and Tabasco sauce.
4. Stir gelatin into sour cream mixture.
5. Pour into greased 2-cup mold. Chill until firm.
6. Unmold and serve with crackers or raw vegetables.

Scampi Salad

Serves 8

A complete meal — serve with homemade bread.

4 cups fresh spinach leaves, torn
8 ounces kidney beans, drained
1 8-ounce can garbanzo beans, drained
1 8-ounce can water chestnuts, drained and sliced
1 cup mushrooms, sliced
⅓ cup Bermuda onion, sliced
2 cloves garlic, crushed
¼ cup plus 2 tablespoons Italian salad dressing
1 pound fresh shrimp, peeled and deveined
4 hard-boiled eggs, peeled and quartered
4 1-ounce slices Swiss cheese, cut in triangles
2 medium tomatoes, cut in wedges

1. In a large bowl combine spinach, kidney beans, garbanzo beans, water chestnuts, mushrooms and onion.
2. Add garlic to Italian dressing. Pour ¼ cup dressing over vegetables and toss. Cover and chill.
3. Cook shrimp in boiling water 3 to 4 minutes. Drain and set aside to cool.
4. To serve, cover serving platter with salad ingredients.
5. Arrange eggs, cheese and tomatoes around edge of platter.
6. Place shrimp on top and drizzle with remaining 2 tablespoons of salad dressing.

Victory Salad

Serves 8 to 10

A multi-talented recipe.

6 tomatoes, chopped
2 cucumbers, peeled and chopped
1 medium red onion, chopped
1 green pepper, chopped
1 can pitted ripe olives, drained and sliced
4 ounces Feta cheese, crumbled
⅓ cup olive oil
¼ cup red wine vinegar
¼ cup fresh parsley, minced
2 cloves garlic, crushed
1 tablespoon sugar
1 teaspoon basil
½ teaspoon oregano
½ teaspoon black pepper

1. Place vegetables and cheese in a large bowl.
2. Shake remaining ingredients in a jar and pour over vegetables.
3. Toss well.

Serve at room temperture. Serve over Romaine as a salad, over hot pasta as a sauce, or in pita halves as a sandwich.

Baked Butternut Squash Soup

Serves 4 to 6

Just as flavorful served cold.

2 butternut squash, about 1 pound each, peeled, seeded and cut into 1-inch pieces
2 carrots, peeled and cut into ½-inch pieces
1 medium onion, finely chopped
3 cups chicken broth
2 teaspoons honey
⅛ teaspoon mace
⅛ teaspoon ground ginger
⅛ teaspoon cinnamon
⅛ teaspoon allspice
¼ teaspoon salt
¼ teaspoon pepper
4 sprigs parsley, without stems, chopped fine

1. Preheat oven to 400°.
2. Place squash, carrots and onion in a shallow casserole dish.
3. Pour broth over vegetables.
4. Drizzle with honey.
5. Add mace, ginger, cinnamon, allspice, salt and pepper.
6. Cover dish with aluminum foil and bake for 45 to 50 minutes.
7. Allow to cool slightly.
8. Place vegetables and broth in blender and purée until smooth.
9. Pass purée through a sieve into a stockpot.
10. Slowly bring to a boil over medium-low heat.
11. Ladle into bowls and garnish with parsley.

Lentil and Brown Rice Soup

Serves 8 to 10

A nutritious, low fat, complete meal.

3 carrots, peeled and chopped
1 onion, chopped
1 stalk celery, chopped
3 cloves garlic, crushed
1 tablespoon corn oil
3 cups water
1½ cups lentils, rinsed and picked over
1 cup brown rice
1 16-ounce can stewed tomatoes, chopped
½ teaspoon basil
½ teaspoon oregano
1 bay leaf
5 cups chicken stock
½ cup fresh parsley, chopped
2 tablespoons cider vinegar
1 teaspoon salt
¼ teaspoon pepper

1. In a large stockpot over medium heat, sauté carrots, onion, celery and garlic in oil.
2. Add water, lentils, rice, tomatoes, basil, oregano, bay leaf and stock.
3. Bring to boil, lower heat and simmer, covered, stirring occasionally for 45 to 55 minutes until rice and lentils are tender.
4. Stir in parsley, vinegar, salt and pepper.
5. Discard bay leaf before serving.

Serve hot in bowls or mugs with whole grain bread.

Siss-Boom-Bah Soup

Serves 4 to 6

The hint of gin makes this soup something to cheer about.

2 cups chicken broth
2 cups clam juice
2 cups half-and-half
2 tablespoons fresh parsley, chopped
2 tablespoons fresh chives, chopped
1 tablespoon fresh dill, chopped
½ teaspoon onion powder
½ teaspoon celery salt
3 tablespoons cornstarch
½ cup gin

1. In a large saucepan, mix all ingredients except cornstarch and gin. Bring to a boil, stirring constantly.
2. In a small bowl, mix together 2 cups of hot liquid with cornstarch. Stir until thickened.
3. Return cornstarch mixture to saucepan, stirring constantly.
4. Add gin and return to boiling. Reduce heat and let soup simmer 5 minutes.
5. Pour into heated thermos or let cool and serve at room temperature.

Pigskin Pies

Serves 12

No spiking allowed!

Filling:

1 cup frozen hash brown potatoes
2 cups (about 1 pound) pork,
  uncooked and ground
1 small onion, chopped
¼ cup carrot, grated
¼ cup turnip, finely chopped
1 clove garlic, crushed
½ teaspoon salt
½ teaspoon black pepper, ground

Pastry:

4 cups flour
1 teaspoon salt
1 cup (2 sticks) butter
1 cup ice water
½ cup butter, melted

Filling preparation:

1. Combine all ingredients in large bowl. Stir until well blended.
2. Cover and refrigerate until ready to use.

Pastry preparation:

1. Preheat oven to 375°.
2. Add salt to flour. Using a pastry blender, cut butter into flour mixture until it resembles coarse meal.
3. Slowly add water, mixing until a soft dough forms.
4. Turn dough onto a lightly floured surface.
5. Roll out dough, using a floured rolling pin, to ⅛-inch thickness.
6. Cut pastry into 24 football shapes by hand or with cookie cutter.
7. Transfer half of shapes to a greased baking sheet.

Assembly:

1. Spoon 2 tablespoons of filling on top of each football shape. Place remaining football shapes over filling.
2. To seal crimp edges with fork.
3. Score tops of pastry to resemble the seams of a football.
4. Brush tops with melted butter.
5. Bake 35 to 40 minutes or until golden brown.
6. When done wrap in heavy duty foil and bring to football game or transfer to wire rack to cool completely.

Baked Grits

Serves 8 to 10

Memories of Charleston.

1 cup grits
1 teaspoon salt
4 cups water
½ cup butter
¼ pound process cheese spread
3 eggs, slightly beaten
⅓ cup milk

1. Preheat oven to 325°.
2. In a medium saucepan cook grits in salted water until done (about 5 minutes).
3. Add butter, cheese spread, eggs and milk. Stir until cheese is melted and mixture is smooth.
4. Place in a 2-quart greased baking pan.
5. Bake 1 hour.

Serve hot as a side dish.

Franks And Beans

Serves 6 to 8

When you don't have time to grill the hot dogs, this is a suitable alternative.

4 foot long or 8 regular hot dogs, chopped in ¾-inch pieces
1 small onion, chopped fine
2 16-ounce cans "barbecue" style baked beans
2 16-ounce cans "homestyle" or regular baked beans
2 tablespoons ketchup
1 tablespoon mustard
2 teaspoons brown sugar
1 tablespoon vegetable oil

1. In large frypan cook hot dog pieces in oil until brown.
2. Add onion and cook until soft.
3. Add remaining ingredients and mix well.
4. Cook 5 minutes or until heated through.

Improves with age — great as leftovers!
Add crushed pineapple for a different flavor.

Extra Point Peas

Serves 4 to 6

1 package frozen peas
2 tablespoons butter
2 tablespoons scallions, chopped
1 tablespoon dried dill
2 tablespoons pimento, chopped
½ cup Swiss cheese, shredded (Jarlsberg may be substituted)

1. Cook peas as directed on package.
2. Melt butter in separate pan.
3. Sauté scallions in butter for 2 minutes.
4. Stir in cooked peas, dill and pimento.
5. Pour into serving dish and top with cheese.
6. Serve immediately.

Lenore's Team Color Cookies

Makes 4 dozen

Go Team Go!

1 cup (2 sticks) butter
½ cup brown sugar
2 egg yolks
2 cups flour
2 egg whites
2 cups walnuts, finely ground

1. Preheat oven to 350°.
2. Cream together butter, sugar and egg yolks.
3. Add 2 cups flour. Mix and knead gently.
4. Beat 2 egg whites until frothy. Set aside.
5. Place 2 cups finely ground walnuts in bowl. Set aside.
6. Roll dough into 1-inch balls.
7. Roll balls in egg whites and then into walnuts.
8. Place on ungreased cookie sheet. Make indentation in center of each cookie with thumb.
9. Bake for 8 minutes.
10. Remove cookies from oven. Press centers again, with back of teaspoon.
11. Cool cookies on wire rack.

Frosting:

3 tablespoon butter, softened
3 cups confectioner's sugar
1 teaspoon vanilla
¼ cup milk
food coloring

Frosting preparation:

1. Cream butter and sugar.
2. Add vanilla and enough milk to blend to a fluffy consistency. Divide in half.
3. Color each according to your "team colors." With pastry bag tip or teaspoon, dollop each cookie with frosting. Cookies may be frozen at this point.

Rules for eating:
Before game — eat cookies with your team colors only or game is jinxed.
After game — losers must eat winning team color cookies.

162

Jelly Roll Cake

Serves 10 to 12

3 eggs
1 cup sugar
1 cup flour
1 teaspoon baking powder
½ teaspoon vanilla
½ cup confectioner's sugar
1 cup raspberry preserves

1. Preheat oven to 350°.
2. In a large bowl, beat eggs until light.
3. Gradually add sugar, while continuing to beat.
4. Sift flour and baking powder together over bowl. Mix with eggs and sugar.
5. Add vanilla and stir.
6. Pour into greased and floured jellyroll pan.
7. Bake 10 minutes.
8. Remove from oven and cool on wire rack 5 minutes.
9. Sprinkle cake with confectioner's sugar.
10. Cover cake with wax paper and immediately invert. (Wax paper is now under cake.)
11. Spread entire surface of cake with raspberry preserves and immediately roll from short end of cake.
12. Let cool, seam side down, on wax paper.

Molasses Cake

Makes 24 2-inch squares

Traditional New England recipe.

1 cup sugar
1 cup molasses
½ teaspoon cinnamon
1 teaspoon ginger
½ teaspoon nutmeg
¼ teaspoon cloves
¼ teaspoon salt
1½ cups warm water
½ cup (1 stick) butter
2 teaspoons baking soda
4 cups flour
raisins (optional)

1. Preheat oven to 350°.
2. Grease 9x13-inch pan.
3. In a large bowl mix together sugar, molasses, cinnamon, ginger, nutmeg, cloves and salt.
4. Add warm water, butter, baking soda and flour. Mix thoroughly.
5. Add raisins if desired.
6. Pour into pan and bake for 30 minutes.
7. Cool in pan on wire rack.

Serve with a glass of milk in winter or lemonade in summer.

Scottish Shortbread

Makes 3 dozen

Handed down through four generations.

1 pound butter, unsalted
1 cup sugar
6 cups flour

1. Soften butter to room temperature. DO NOT melt butter, this will alter texture. Place butter and sugar in a mixing bowl and thoroughly blend to a creamy consistency.
2. Slowly add 4 cups flour, one cup at a time and blend until flour is completely incorporated.
3. Add remaining flour by hand.
4. Place dough on a lightly floured surface and knead for 2 to 3 minutes until dough is nice and smooth.
5. Shape dough into a small brick-shaped loaf, 10x4x2-inches.
6. Refrigerate.
7. Preheat oven to 325°.
8. Slice off 2-inch squares that are ¼-inch thick.
9. Place on cookie sheet.
10. Bake for 20 minutes or until edges begin to brown slightly.
11. When cookies have cooled, frost with Butter Frosting.

Butter Frosting:

½ cup (1 stick) butter
1 pound box confectioner's sugar
1 teaspoon vanilla
1 to 2 teaspoons milk
walnut halves

Butter Frosting preparation:

1. Mix butter, sugar and vanilla in a mixing bowl until well blended and smooth. Add 1 to 2 teaspoons of milk if too thick.
2. Ice top of each cookie and place a walnut half in center.

Sweet Cheese Dip For Fruit
Makes 3½ cups

Serve in a real fruit container, such as a hollowed-out pineapple.

2 8-ounce packages cream cheese
1 7-ounce jar marshmallow creme
¼ cup milk
1½ teaspoons vanilla
½ teaspoon ground nutmeg
assorted fruits

1. In a medium bowl combine all ingredients except fruits. Beat until smooth.
2. Place dip in serving bowl and arrange fruit around bowl.

Coach's Hot Spiked Mocha Coffee

Wrap hands around coffee mug to keep them warm.

strong brewed coffee
instant hot chocolate powder
Kahlúa
1 can whipped cream (optional)

1. Brew coffee for all tailgate picnickers.
2. To each mug of coffee, add 2 tablespoons instant hot cocoa mix and 1 tablespoon Kahlúa.
3. Top with whipped cream and serve.

Harvey Wallbanger Slush
Serves 6

Drink slowly to avoid falling off the bench.

5 cups orange juice
¾ cup vodka
⅓ cup Galliano liqueur
orange slices
maraschino cherries

1. In large bowl, mix orange juice, vodka and Galliano. Stir to mix well.
2. Pour into 2-quart freezer container. Freeze 6 hours or overnight. Mixture will not freeze firm.
3. To serve, spoon into stemmed glasses and garnish with an orange slice and a cherry.

HAYRIDE OR SLEIGHRIDE

SAMPLE MENU

Voyager Artichoke Soup

Wagon Wheel Bread

Happy Trails Salad

Barnsider Brownies

Hot Mulled Cider

Piling people together for a hayride or sleighride provides a magnificent opportunity to blend beautiful landscapes with congenial companions. With today's busy schedules, it is a real treat to settle back blissfully and let old-fashioned horsepower carry us far from everyday cares. Pack imaginative picnics for these joyful journeys. Your party will "ooh and aah" as you reveal layer after layer of luscious cuisine prepared to complement your enjoyable escape.

Hot Maryland Crab Dip

Makes 3 cups

Even the crabbiest of guests will love this dip.

1 8-ounce package cream cheese
1 cup sour cream
2 tablespoons mayonnaise
2 teaspoons Worcestershire sauce
1 teaspoon dry mustard
1 teaspoon garlic powder
½ cup cheddar cheese, grated
1 pound fresh crabmeat,
    OR 2 cans crabmeat, drained,
    OR 1 package frozen crabmeat, thawed

1. Preheat oven to 325°.
2. Cream the cream cheese until soft.
3. Add the remaining ingredients to this, except for crabmeat. Blend well.
4. Fold in the crabmeat.
5. Put mixture in a baking dish and bake for 30 minutes.

Serve hot with favorite crackers or crusty bread pieces.

Mini Magic Meatballs

Makes 4 dozen

The sauce performs the magic.

1 pound ground beef
2 cups white bread, torn into small pieces
1 package dry onion soup mix
1 egg, slightly beaten
1 tablespoon parsley flakes

1. Preheat oven to 350°.
2. In a large mixing bowl combine ground beef, bread, dried soup mix, egg and parsley.
3. Shape into 1-inch balls and arrange in a glass baking dish.
4. Make Magic Sauce (below) and pour over meatballs. Bake uncovered for 45 minutes.
5. Spoon off excess fat before serving.

Magic Sauce:
1 cup ketchup
⅓ cup lemon juice
⅓ cup grape jelly

Magic Sauce preparation:

1. Blend ketchup, lemon juice and jelly together.

Meatballs can be placed on wax paper in pans and frozen. Remove from pans and store in freezer bags until needed.

Happy Trails Salad

This is pretty, zesty and always popular.

2 12-ounce packages tricolor tortellini
2 12-ounce bags frozen mixed vegetables
   (broccoli, cauliflower and carrots)
3 cups Robusto salad dressing
2 cups pepperoni, sliced
1 cup Parmesan cheese

1. Boil tortellini until tender (5 to 7 minutes.)
2. Pour boiling water over frozen vegetables to thaw. Strain.
3. In a large bowl combine tortellini and vegetables. Add salad dressing and pepperoni.
4. Chill several hours.
5. Just before serving sprinkle on Parmesan cheese.

Veggie Pasta Salad

Serves 6 to 8

All you need to remember — 8 ounces pasta, ¾ cup each veggy and ½ cup dressing. What could be easier?

8 ounces macaroni shells, cooked
¾ cup cucumber, chopped
¾ cup green pepper, chopped
¾ cup scallions, sliced
¾ cup tomatoes, chopped
¾ cup black olives, chopped
¾ cup broccoli, chopped
½ cup Italian dressing

1. Toss all ingredients together and serve.
2. Serve at once or cover and refrigerate until ready to serve.

Voyager Artichoke Soup

Serves 4 to 6

1 cup scallions, sliced
¼ cup onions, chopped
2 tablespoons butter, melted
2 tablespoons flour
1½ quarts chicken broth
1 14-ounce can artichoke hearts,
   drained and chopped
¼ teaspoon white pepper
2 tablespoons fresh parsley, minced

Can be made ahead. Cover and chill. Reheat to serve.

1. In a large saucepan over medium heat, sauté scallions and onions in butter until tender.
2. Add flour and cook 1 minute, stirring constantly.
3. Add broth and stir until thickened.
4. Add artichoke hearts and white pepper.
5. Cook until thoroughly heated.
6. Serve sprinkled with fresh parsley.

Scandinavian Vegetable And Shrimp Soup   Serves 8

Serve this soup for a very special occasion.

1 pound peas, frozen
1 head cauliflower, cut into florets
2 potatoes, peeled and diced to ½-inch
4 radishes, quartered
4 small carrots, peeled and diced to ½-inch
1 teaspoon salt
1 10-ounce package frozen
  chopped spinach, thawed
2 tablespoons butter
2 tablespoons flour
1 cup milk
1 egg yolk
¼ cup heavy cream
3 tablespoons cooking sherry
1 pound shrimp, cleaned and cooked

1. Place peas, cauliflower, potatoes, radishes and carrots in a 5-quart stockpot.
2. Cover vegetables with cold water. Add salt and boil for 5 minutes.
3. Add spinach and cook another 5 minutes. Remove from heat.
4. Strain vegetables to separate them from liquid. Keep vegetables and liquid in separate bowls.
5. In stockpot melt butter over moderate heat. Remove from heat and stir in flour. Slowly pour in hot vegetable stock beating vigorously with a wire whisk and then beat in milk.
6. In a small bowl combine egg yolk and cream and slowly add 1 cup of hot stock.
7. Slowly whisk egg mixture into stock. Add sherry, vegetables and shrimp.
8. Salt and pepper to taste.

Aunt Pat's Special Sandwiches   Serves 12

1 pound salami, diced
12 ounces sharp yellow cheddar cheese, diced
1 4-ounce jar pimento, chopped
1 8-ounce can black olives, drained and chopped
2 teaspoons Worcestershire sauce
1 medium onion, chopped
15 to 20 hot dog rolls

Requires some advance preparation.

1. In a large bowl mix together salami, cheese, pimento, olives, Worcestershire sauce and onion. Refrigerate overnight.
2. When ready to serve, Preheat oven to 325°.
3. Fill hot dog rolls and place in 13x9x2-inch pan close together.
4. Bake 15 to 20 minutes until cheese is melted.

Serve hot or cold.

Clam Bisque

One of the *best* bisques.

1 cup onion, chopped
½ cup (1 stick) butter
6 tablespoons flour
3 8-ounce cans minced clams with liquid
2 8-ounce bottles clam juice
3 cups light cream
3 tablespoons lemon juice

Soup may be made ahead . . . . chilled and reheated in double boiler over low heat.

1. In large pot sauté onion in butter until soft. Stir in flour. Cook, stirring constantly until bubbly and smooth.
2. Stir in clams with liquid and clam juice. Continue cooking and stirring until mixture thickens. Boil 1 minute. Cover and reduce heat.
3. Simmer 15 minutes to blend flavors.
4. Blend in cream and lemon juice and stir until heated.

Taco Casserole

Serves 6 to 8

This is especially popular with young, hungry eaters.

2 pounds ground beef
1 packet, dry taco seasoning
⅔ large box tortilla chips
1 pound cheddar cheese, grated
2 large tomatoes, chopped
½ head lettuce, chopped
1 onion, chopped
1 cup sour cream
1 cup salsa
1 cup quacamole

1. Preheat oven to 350°.
2. In large frypan, brown ground beef. Drain fat. Add seasoning and stir.
3. In a 9x13-inch casserole layer tortilla chips with beef on top.
4. On top of this put cheese, tomatoes, lettuce and onion.
5. Bake for about 15 minutes until heated through and cheese is melted.
6. Serve with sour cream, salsa (Lynn Anderson's — see index) and quacamole (see index).

If you prefer, just bake beef, chips and cheese and let people spoon other ingredients on top. OR don't bake at all! Cook beef and taco seasoning according to taco mix directions. Keep warm and place all other ingredients in a separate bowl. Let everyone "Make Their Own Casserole" by layering any or all ingredients into their own individual plates.

Beef And Bean Casserole

Serves 10 to 12

1 large onion, chopped
1 green pepper, chopped
2 tablespoons butter
1 pound ground beef
2 16-ounce cans pork and beans
⅓ cup brown sugar
½ cup barbecue sauce
1 cup cheddar cheese, grated

**Option: If you are making this at home:
20 minutes before it is done, cut refrigerator
biscuits in half and place cut side down on
top of casserole. Continue baking.**

1. Preheat oven to 350°.
2. In a large saucepan sauté onion and green
   pepper in butter until lightly browned.
3. Stir in ground beef and cook until no
   longer pink. Drain off fat.
4. Add pork and beans, brown sugar
   and barbecue sauce. Pour into large
   casserole dish.
5. Sprinkle cheese on top.
6. Bake for 45 minutes.

Serve hot.

Wagon Wheel Bread

Makes 1 flat bread

Dough, rolled thinner, can be used for pizza.

1 cup warm water
3 tablespoons olive oil
1 package dry yeast
3½ cups flour, all white
   OR half white and half whole wheat
1 teaspoon salt
2 tablespoons cornmeal
herbs (optional)
chopped ham (optional)

**Optional ingredients may be mixed into dough
before kneading.**

1. In large bowl, mix water, olive oil
   and yeast.
2. Add 2 cups flour and the salt
   and mix well.
3. Stir in remaining flour until dough
   forms a ball.
4. Knead dough on floured surface until
   it becomes smooth and elastic, adding
   flour to prevent stickiness.
5. Place dough in greased bowl and turn
   to grease both sides.
6. Cover bowl with cloth and let rise until
   doubled — 1 hour.
7. Preheat oven to 400°. Place baking
   stone or cookie sheet in oven to heat.
8. Punch dough down and form into ball
   on a floured surface.
9. Flatten into a rough circle or rectangle
   about ¾-inch thick.
10. Place dough on the flat, back side
    of a cookie sheet sprinkled with
    2 tablespoons corn meal.

11. With fingers punch dimples in dough.
12. Brush with olive oil.
13. Slide dough off cookie sheet onto hot baking stone or cookie sheet in oven.
14. Bake for 20 minutes until lightly browned.

Serve hot or cold.

Barnsider Brownies

Outstanding recipe!

Makes 16 2-inch squares

Cheese layer:
1 3-ounce package cream cheese
2 tablespoons butter
¼ cup sugar
1 egg
1 tablespoon flour
½ teaspoon vanilla

Chocolate layer:
1 4-ounce package sweet chocolate
3 tablespoons butter
2 eggs
¾ cup sugar
½ teaspoon baking powder
¼ teaspoon salt
½ cup flour
1 teaspoon vanilla
¼ teaspoon almond extract
½ cup nuts, chopped

Cheese layer preparation:
1. In a small bowl, cream together cream cheese and butter.
2. Gradually add sugar, creaming until fluffy.
3. Blend in egg, flour and vanilla. Set aside.

Chocolate layer preparation:
1. In a small saucepan, melt chocolate and butter over very low heat. Stir and set aside to cool.
2. In a large bowl, beat eggs until light.
3. Slowly add sugar, beating until thickened.
4. Add baking powder, salt and flour.
5. Blend in cooled chocolate mixture.
6. Add vanilla, almond extract and nuts. Mix well.

Assembly:
1. Preheat oven to 350°.
2. Spread half the chocolate batter in a greased 8-inch square pan.
3. Top with cheese mixture.
4. Spoon remaining chocolate batter over cheese layer.
5. Zigzag knife through batter to marble.
6. Bake 35 to 40 minutes.
7. Cool, in pan, on wire rack.

Mom's Traditional Apple Pie

Serves 8 to 10

Crust:

2 cups flour
1½ teaspoons sugar
1 cup (2 sticks) butter
¼ cup cold water

1. In a medium bowl, combine flour and sugar.
2. Cut in butter with a pastry blender until incorporated.
3. Gradually add water, mixing with a fork. Dough will be somewhat dry.
4. Separate dough into 2 halves.
5. Wrap each half in wax paper and refrigerate at least 30 minutes or overnight.

Filling:

½ cup corn flakes, crumbled
8 Macintosh apples
½ cup sugar
1 teaspoon cinnamon
½ cup raisins
½ cup walnuts, chopped
2 tablespoons butter

Filling preparation:

1. Preheat oven to 350°.
2. Grease entire inside of 9-inch pie plate with butter.
3. Roll out 1 package refrigerated dough on floured surface with floured rolling pin making sure rolled dough is large enough to overlap sides of 9-inch pie plate.
4. Place dough into pie plate.
5. Layer corn flakes over bottom crust.
6. Peel, core and slice apples into 1- to 1½-inch pieces.
7. Place apples on top of corn flakes.
8. Mix sugar, cinnamon, raisins and walnuts together and sprinkle over apples.
9. Dot with butter.
10. Roll out second package refrigerated dough.
11. Fit crust over filled pie. Pinch edges closed with fingers.
12. Pierce 5 or 6 slits into crust with knife.
13. Bake 45 to 50 minutes.
14. Allow to stand 30 minutes before slicing and serving.

Nutmeg Loaf Cake

Makes one loaf

1 cup sugar
½ cup (1 stick) butter
1 egg
2 cups flour
2 teaspoons baking powder
1 teaspoon nutmeg
1 cup milk
½ cup raisins
½ cup walnuts
1 teaspoon vinegar

1. Preheat oven to 350°.
2. Grease 9x5x3-inch loaf pan.
3. Cream together sugar and butter.
4. Add egg. Mix well.
5. Stir in flour, baking powder and nutmeg.
6. Add milk. Mix well.
7. Add raisins and nuts.
8. Just before putting into loaf pan, add 1 teaspoon vinegar.
9. Bake for 1¼ hours. When toothpick inserted into cake comes out clean, cake is done.
10. Cool on rack in pan 10 minutes. Remove cake from pan and continue to cool.

Serve warm or cold.

Pecan Tarts

Makes 24 tarts

Dough:
1 4-ounce package cream cheese, softened
½ cup (1 stick) butter, softened
1 cup flour

Filling:
1 egg
¾ cup dark brown sugar
1 teaspoon vanilla
1 cup pecans, chopped
24 pecan halves

Hint: After shaping dough into balls, place in muffin cups. With a cork (from a wine bottle) that has been dipped in flour, press down on dough. Cork will make a well in the center, and dough will be pushed up and around the sides, leaving you with a tart shell.

1. In a medium bowl beat together cream cheese and butter.
2. Mix in flour until dough forms a ball.
3. Cover and chill 1 hour.
4. Preheat oven to 325°.
5. Shape dough into 24 1-inch balls.
6. Press balls into bottom and sides of 1½-inch diameter muffin cups. (See hint left.) Set aside.
7. In a medium bowl beat together egg, sugar and vanilla until smooth.
8. Add chopped nuts and mix.
9. Fill muffin cups with mixture.
10. Place a pecan half on top of each cup.
11. Bake 25 minutes.
12. Cool in pan on wire rack.

GHOST HUNTING

SAMPLE MENU

Floating Ghost

Graveyard Ghoulash

Spirit Risen Bread

Death By Chocolate

Booberry Pie

Café Diable

Make no bones about it; the cemetery is a peaceful and interesting place to visit. Casual strolls among the stones can be very entertaining as you read the cleverly written epitaphs and familiarize yourself with local history. If you don't have a ghost of an idea about what type of food you should be "goblin," we've provided some breathtaking choices. But you must choose wisely "boocause" some are so tantalizing, they might . . . . *shhh* . . . . *lift the spirits.*

Floating Ghost

Serves 4 to 6

1 cup sesame seeds, toasted
2 tablespoons butter
1 8-ounce package cream cheese
½ cup soy sauce
mini-rice crackers

1. Toast sesame seeds in butter and spread on waxed paper.
2. Coat the block of cream cheese with sesame seeds.
3. "Float" the sesame coated cheese in the soy sauce which has been poured into a dish with slightly raised sides.

Serve with rice crackers.

Zucchini Bites

Makes 48 bites

3 cups zucchini, unpared but shredded
1 cup buttermilk baking mix
½ cup onion, grated
½ cup Parmesan cheese
2 tablespoons parsley
½ teaspoon salt
½ teaspoon seasoned salt
½ teaspoon oregano
dash pepper
1 clove garlic, crushed
½ cup vegetable oil
4 eggs, slightly beaten

1. Preheat oven to 350°.
2. Mix all ingredients.
3. Spread in greased 9x13-inch pan.
4. Bake for 25 minutes until golden brown.
5. Cool 5 minutes before cutting into 1½-inch squares.

Serve hot or at room temperature.

Cranberry Turkey Salad

Serves 4 to 6

Another recipe idea for Thanksgiving leftovers.

2 cups cooked turkey, cubed
½ cup seedless green grapes, halved
1 tablespoon lemon juice
¾ cup celery, diced
2 eggs, hard-boiled and chopped

1. In a large bowl, toss turkey, grapes and lemon juice together.
2. Add celery and eggs. Mix gently.
3. In a separate bowl, blend mayonnaise, cranberry sauce, salt and basil; toss lightly with turkey mixture.
4. Chill.
5. Fold in nuts, just before serving.

Dressing:

½ cup mayonnaise
½ cup canned whole cranberry sauce
½ teaspoon salt
¼ teaspoon basil
¼ teaspoon slivered almonds, toasted

Dilled Potato Salad

Serves 4 to 6

Is it the wine that makes the difference?

1 pound small red potatoes
¼ teaspoon Dijon mustard
1 tablespoon white wine vinegar
½ teaspoon dry white wine
2 tablespoons olive oil
¼ cup fresh dill, minced

May be made ahead and chilled, but return to room temperature before serving.

1. Scrub potatoes and cut lengthwise into quarters.
2. In pan, steam potatoes covered for 7 to 10 minutes or until tender.
3. In a bowl, whisk the mustard, vinegar, white wine and oil until emulsified.
4. Add potatoes to the dressing while they are still warm. Toss gently.
5. Sprinkle on the dill and let salad stand 30 minutes.

Serve at room temperature.

Split-Pea And Barley Soup

Serves 4 to 6

Couldn't be easier.

5 cups chicken broth
3½ cups water
1½ cups dried split peas, rinsed and drained
½ cup barley
1 large carrot, diced
½ cup onion, chopped
1 large stalk celery, diced
1 teaspoon garlic, crushed
¼ teaspoon thyme
¼ teaspoon white pepper

1. Put all ingredients in a 3- to 4-quart pot.
2. Bring to a boil.
3. Reduce heat and simmer uncovered about 1 hour. Peas will begin to fall apart when cooked.

Minestrone Soup

Serves 10 to 12

½ cup (1 stick) butter
2 cups zucchini, unpeeled but diced
2 cups carrots, peeled and sliced
2 cups potatoes, peeled and diced
⅔ cups celery, thinly sliced
3 slices bacon
1 cup onions, chopped
3 quarts chicken broth
1 tablespoon dry parsley
4 cups canned tomatoes,
   drained and chopped
1 bay leaf
1 teaspoon salt
½ teaspoon pepper
1 cup white rice
2 cans red kidney beans, drained

1. Melt butter in large frypan. Add zucchini, carrots, potatoes and celery, tossing to coat. Cook for 5 minutes. Set aside.
2. Cook bacon in 8-quart stockpot until browned. Lift out with slotted spoon and drain on paper towel. Set aside and dice when cool.
3. Discard most of the bacon fat in the pot.
4. Add to pot: chopped onions and vegetables from the frypan, chicken broth, parsley, tomatoes, bay leaf, salt and pepper. Bring soup to boil. Reduce heat, partially cover and simmer 25 minutes.
5. Remove and discard bay leaf.
6. Add rice, red kidney beans, diced cooked bacon and cook 15 to 20 minutes longer.

Serve with chopped parsley or chopped garlic and grated cheese.

Graveyard Ghoulash

Serves 4 to 6

1½ cups elbow macaroni
1 pound ground beef
1 large onion, chopped
2 cloves garlic, crushed
1 medium green pepper, chopped
1 28-ounce can whole tomatoes
1 4½-ounce can tomato paste
1 8-ounce can sliced mushrooms, undrained
2 teaspoons chili pepper
1 teaspoon sugar
¾ teaspoon basil
½ teaspoon oregano
1 teaspoon salt
½ teaspoon pepper
1 large bay leaf, whole
½ cup Parmesan cheese

1. In large pot, boil water for macaroni. Add macaroni and cook 10 to 12 minutes until done. Drain.
2. In large frypan brown beef. Then drain off excess fat.
3. Add onion, garlic and green pepper. Cook until soft.
4. Add tomatoes, paste and mushrooms with liquid plus all seasonings.
5. Mix well. Reduce heat to simmer. Cover and cook 30 minutes.
6. Add cooked macaroni. Mix well. Cover and cook an additional 5 minutes.
7. Serve in bowls with a sprinkle of Parmesan cheese on top.

Improves with age as a leftover.

Spirit Risen Bread

Makes 2 loaves

Eating this wonderful bread will lift your spirits.

2 packages dry yeast
½ cup water
1½ cups boiling water
1 cup quick cooking oats
⅓ cup butter
½ cup molasses
4 teaspoons salt
2 eggs, beaten
5½ cups flour
melted butter

1. In small bowl soften yeast in ½ cup lukewarm water.
2. In a large bowl combine 1½ cups boiling water, oats, butter, molasses and salt. Cool to lukewarm.
3. Add softened yeast. Mix well.
4. Blend in eggs.
5. Add flour and mix thoroughly until dough is blended. It will be softer than bread dough that is kneaded.
6. Place in greased bowl and turn dough to grease surface.
7. Cover and store in refrigerator at least 2 hours.
8. Preheat oven to 350°.
9. Shape dough into two loaves on well floured board.
10. Place into two greased standard loaf pans (9x5-inches).
11. Rub top with melted butter and bake for 45 minutes.
12. When done remove bread from pan and cool on rack.

Zucchini Bread

Makes 2 loaves

The most versatile of all vegetables, the zucchini.

3 eggs, lightly beaten
1½ cups sugar
1 cup oil
2 cups zucchini, grated
2 teaspoons vanilla
2 cups flour
¼ teaspoon baking powder
2 teaspoons baking soda
1 tablespoon cinnamon
1 teaspoon salt
1 cup nuts (optional)
1 cup raisins (optional)

1. Preheat oven to 375°.
2. In a large bowl beat together eggs and sugar.
3. Blend in oil, zucchini and vanilla.
4. In separate bowl, mix together flour, baking powder, baking soda, cinnamon and salt.
5. Add to egg mixture and mix thoroughly.
6. Add nuts and/or raisins, if desired.
7. Pour into 2 9x5x3-inch greased and floured loaf pans.
8. Bake 50 to 60 minutes.
9. Cool in pan on wire rack, 5 minutes. Remove bread to rack and continue to cool.

Lemon Tea Fingers

Makes 39 pieces

Your fingers will keep reaching for more of these sensational cookies.

¾ cup (1½ sticks) butter
¾ cup confectioner's sugar
1½ cups flour
2 eggs
1 cup brown sugar
2 tablespoons flour
½ teaspoon baking powder
½ teaspoon salt
1 teaspoon vanilla
1 cup walnuts or pecans, chopped

Variation: Ice with orange lemon icing:
1½ cups confectioner's sugar
2 teaspoons butter, melted
1 tablespoon orange juice
1 teaspoon lemon juice

1. Preheat oven to 350°.
2. In medium bowl, cream butter and confectioner's sugar. Blend in flour.
3. Press evenly in bottom of ungreased 13x9x2-inch baking pan. Bake 12 to 15 minutes.
4. In bowl mix remaining ingredients and spread over hot baked layer. Bake 20 minutes or longer.
5. Cool and cut into 1x3-inch bars.

Variation:
1. Blend all ingredients until smooth and spreadable.
2. Spread on warm bars before cutting.

Mince Meat Coffee Cake

Serves 10 to 12

¾ cup (1½ sticks) butter, softened
2 cups flour
¾ cup sugar
2½ teaspoons baking powder
½ teaspoon salt
I egg
I cup mincemeat
¾ cup milk

1. Preheat oven to 350°.
2. Grease an 8-inch angelfood pan.
3. In a large bowl, mix butter with flour, sugar, baking powder and salt.
4. In a medium bowl mix egg, mincemeat and milk. Add to dry ingredients. Blend well.
5. Place in well greased angelfood pan.
6. Bake for 30 minutes or until done. Glaze.

Glaze:

¾ cup confectioner's sugar
2 tablespoons warm water
½ teaspoon almond extract

Glaze preparation:

Mix together all ingredients. Pour over top of coffee cake while cake is still hot.

Booberry Pie

Serves 8 to 10

The most foolproof blueberry pie you can make.

6 cups (2 pints) blueberries
¼ cup cornstarch
¼ cup cold water
¾ cup boiling water
I cup sugar
¼ teaspoon salt
1½ tablespoons lemon juice
I tablespoon unsalted butter
I 9-inch baked pie shell

1. Wash berries, drain and towel dry. Set aside.
2. In a large saucepan, stir cornstarch into cold water until dissolved.
3. Add boiling water. Stir until smooth.
4. Add sugar, salt and ½ cup berries.
5. Place over low heat and stir. Crush berries. Cook to a low boil (10 minutes).
6. Reduce heat. Cook another 3 to 4 minutes.
7. Remove pan from heat and stir in lemon juice and butter.
8. Add remaining berries to sauce. Stir several times while mixture cools.
9. Spoon filling into baked pie shell.
10. Refrigerate 3 hours before serving.

Great with a dollop of whipped cream on each piece.

Cosmic Carrot Cake

Serves 10

A new twinkle to an old star.

1½ cups granulated sugar
½ cup brown sugar
½ cup (1 stick) butter
¾ cup canola oil
2 cups flour
2 teaspoons baking powder
1 teaspoon baking soda
1 teaspoon salt
1 teaspoon coriander, ground
1 teaspoon ground ginger
4 eggs OR egg substitute
3 cups carrots, grated
1 8-ounce can crushed
  pineapple, drained
1 cup walnuts, chopped
sliced almonds to decorate

1. Preheat oven to 350°.
2. In a large bowl, beat together sugars, butter and oil.
3. In a separate bowl, sift dry ingredients together with spices.
4. Blend dry ingredients into sugar mixture alternating with eggs, stirring well after each addition.
5. Add carrots and pineapple, blending well. Stir in nuts.
6. Line 2 9-inch cake pans with wax paper or parchment.
7. Pour batter into cake pans and bake for 1 hour or until tester comes out clean.
8. Let cakes cool in pans before removing.
9. Frost with Cream Cheese Frosting (see index). Press sliced almonds into cake edges to decorate.

Death By Chocolate

Serves 8 to 10

This cake is, by far, *the* cake for the chocoholic.

1½ cups sugar
½ cup water
2 tablespoons vanilla
8 ounces unsweetened chocolate
4 ounces semi-sweet chocolate
1 cup unsalted butter
5 eggs (room temperature)
confectioner's sugar

1. Grease 9-inch diameter microwave-safe cake pan with at least 1½-inch sides.
2. Line bottom with waxed paper.
3. In a saucepan, bring 1 cup sugar, water and vanilla to boil.
4. Remove from heat and add half of the unsweetened chocolate and half of the semi-sweet chocolate. Stir until smooth.
5. Stir in half of the butter.
6. Add remaining chocolate, stirring until smooth.

7. Add remaining butter and stir until the entire mixture is smooth.
8. Using electric mixer, beat eggs with remaining ½ cup sugar. When thoroughly mixed, beat in melted chocolate mixture.
9. Pour batter into prepared pan.
10. Place in microwave on high (700 watt microwave) for 4 minutes. Stir mixture gently if clumps have formed in middle.
11. Microwave on high for 4 more minutes. If cake still "jiggles" in the center, microwave on half power for 2 more minutes.
12. Allow to cool for 20 minutes.
13. Unmold onto cake plate.
14. Store at room temperature.
15. Prior to serving sprinkle with confectioner's sugar.

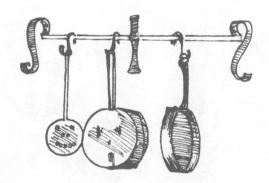

Café Diable
Serves 4

Take the chill out of your bones while drinking this flavorful coffee.

4 cups STRONG black coffee
4 cloves
1 stick cinnamon
1 tablespoon sugar
¼ teaspoon orange rind, grated
1 tablespoon brandy

1. To brewed black coffee add cloves, cinnamon, sugar, orange rind and brandy.
2. Place in heated 1-quart thermos.

Ready to serve when you are.

SKATING & SKIING

SAMPLE MENU

Hot Cider

Salmon Double Axel Cakes

Sunshine and Snow Salad

Warm Up Fruit

Dana's Giant Slalom Cookies

For skating and skiing enthusiasts who thrill to numbing temperatures and frosty skies, the wonders of winter are many and varied. And the foods taken along on such outings can be just as diverse. The stamina needed for gliding across a moonlit pond or whizzing down a snow-covered mountain comes from scrumptious foods that warm and comfort both body and soul. Your iciest outdoor adventures will be even more invigorating if you include some of the following creations for cold weather fanciers.

Sunshine And Snow Salad

Serves 8

A colorful tangy treat.

2 cups fresh orange sections
1 small purple onion, sliced and
　separated into rings
¼ cup red wine vinegar
¼ cup olive oil
2 tablespoons fresh parsley, chopped
8 cups mixed salad greens

1. Combine orange sections and onion rings in a medium bowl; set aside.

2. Combine vinegar and oil; pour over orange mixture and sprinkle with fresh parsley.

3. Cover and chill 3 hours, tossing occasionally.

4. Place salad greens in a shallow dish; arrange orange and onion evenly over greens, and drizzle dressing over salad. Serve immediately.

Oven Stew

Serves 12

4 pounds round steak
　cut into 1-inch cubes
4 cups carrots, sliced
4 cups celery, sliced
4 medium onions, sliced
2 5-ounce cans water chestnuts,
　drained and sliced
2 6-ounce cans sliced mushrooms, drained
¼ cup plus 2 tablespoons flour
2 tablespoons sugar
2 tablespoons salt
2 16-ounce cans tomatoes
2 cups Burgundy wine

2 cups water plus 2 teaspoons instant beef bouillon can be substituted for the Burgundy.

1. Preheat oven to 325°.

2. In roasting pan or 2 stockpots, mix meat, carrots, celery, onions, water chestnuts and mushrooms.

3. In a separate bowl mix flour, sugar and salt and stir into meat mixture.

4. Add tomatoes and Burgundy. Cover.

5. Bake 4 hours or until tender.

Serve with Hot Cran-Apple Cider (see index).

Cheesy Chicken Florentine

Serves 4 to 6

Always requested for a repeat performance.

3 packages frozen chopped spinach,
   thawed and squeezed dry
3 whole chicken breasts, cooked and
   cut into pieces
2 8-ounce packages cream cheese
14 ounces extra sharp
   cheddar cheese, grated
2 cups milk
½ teaspoon salt
½ teaspoon pepper
½ teaspoon dill
½ teaspoon garlic powder
I tablespoon parsley flakes
I cup Parmesan cheese
I cup bread crumbs
¼ cup (½ stick) butter, melted

1. Preheat oven to 375°.
2. Lightly butter 13x9-inch casserole.
3. Line with uncooked spinach.
4. Add chicken. Set aside.
5. Make sauce by melting cream cheese, cheddar cheese, milk, seasonings and ⅔ cup Parmesan cheese. (Reserve ⅓ cup of Parmesan cheese for bread crumb mixture.)
6. Blend over low heat until smooth.
7. Pour cheese sauce over spinach and chicken.
8. Combine bread crumbs with melted butter. Add ⅓ cup Parmesan cheese. Sprinkle mixture on top of mixture.
9. Bake uncovered for 30 minutes.

Chicken With Sausages

Serves 4 to 6

3 whole boneless chicken breasts,
   chopped into bite size pieces
I clove garlic, crushed
2 tablespoons oil
I cup canned crushed tomatoes
½ cup dry white wine
½ cup chicken broth
I teaspoon oregano
I teaspoon basil
6 hot sausages
I cup Mozzarella cheese, shredded

1. In a large stockpot sauté chicken and garlic in oil until browned.
2. Add tomatoes, wine, chicken broth, oregano and basil. Simmer 10 minutes.
3. In a separate pan cook sausages until browned, drain off fat and slice into 1-inch pieces.
4. Preheat oven to 350°.
5. Place sausages and chicken mixture in shallow 10-inch casserole and top with Mozzarella cheese.
6. Bake for 15 to 20 minutes until cheese is bubbly.

Serve hot with Italian bread.

Barbecups

Serves 4 to 6

Tasty cold too.

1 pound ground beef, turkey, or chicken
4 tablespoons onion, minced
½ cup barbecue sauce
2 tablespoons brown sugar
½ teaspoon salt
¼ teaspoon pepper
¼ teaspoon garlic powder
1 can refrigerated biscuit dough
¾ cup cheddar cheese, grated

1. Preheat oven to 400°.
2. In a large frypan brown ground meat and cook onions until translucent.
3. Drain excess fat.
4. Stir in barbecue sauce, sugar, salt, pepper, and garlic powder.
5. Flatten biscuits and place in greased muffin cups, pressing dough in bottom and against sides.
6. Spoon meat mixture into biscuit "cups."
7. Bake 10 to 15 minutes.
8. Sprinkle with cheese and bake until melted.

Can be frozen and reheated.
Leave Barbecups in muffin cups to travel to your picnic destination.

Salmon Double Axel Cakes

Serves 2

The gallery will cheer.

1 6½-ounce can salmon, flaked
1 egg, lightly beaten
¼ cup fresh bread crumbs
2 teaspoons ginger, grated
1 tablespoon shallots, minced
1 tablespoon mayonnaise
¼ teaspoon salt
⅛ teaspoon pepper
1 tablespoon sesame oil
honey mustard
mayonnaise

1. Combine salmon, egg, bread crumbs, ginger, shallots and mayonnaise.
2. Season with salt and pepper.
3. Form into 4 patties.
4. In a medium frypan heat oil. Add patties.
5. Sauté over medium heat until golden on both sides (3 minutes per side).
6. Combine equal parts of honey mustard and mayonnaise. Spread 1 teaspoon of mixture on top of each salmon patty before serving.

These cakes can be made smaller and used as an appetizer. They can also be made ahead and served in a sandwich roll.

Baked Lima Beans

Serves 8 to 10

2 pounds dry lima beans
1 cup (2 sticks) butter
2 cups sugar
1 teaspoon salt
3x2-inch lean salt pork, sliced
   OR about 4 slices bacon

Requires advance preparation.

1. Pick the beans over, wash gently.
2. In a large saucepan cover beans with water. Soak for 12 hours, adding more water if necessary.
3. Preheat oven to 250°.
4. Drain beans and again cover with fresh water. Bring to boil, lower heat and simmer gently for 20 minutes.
5. Remove from heat and drain, reserving liquor.
6. In very large flat pan or 2 9x13-inch pans, place beans with butter, sugar and salt.
7. Cover beans with the liquor and stir gently.
8. Place strips of salt pork or bacon on top.
9. Cover and bake 7 hours. Uncover the last hour so beans will brown on top.

Vegetable Bread

Makes 30 rolls

Easy to serve — Fun to eat — just pull off pieces for individual rolls.

1 cup onion, chopped
½ cup EACH red and
   green pepper, chopped
¾ cup (1½ sticks) butter
½ cup Parmesan cheese, grated
¼ cup bacon, cooked and diced
   OR bacon bits
¼ cup chives
3 cans refrigerator biscuits

1. Preheat oven to 350°.
2. In frypan, sauté onion and peppers in butter until lightly browned.
3. Pour into a large bowl and add Parmesan, bacon and chives.
4. Separate biscuits and toss in bowl with all other ingredients until biscuits are well coated.
5. Layer coated biscuits in greased angelfood pan.
6. Bake for 30 minutes until nicely browned.
7. Invert pan onto serving platter and allow bread to cool.

Reuben Bread

Makes 1 9x5-inch loaf

1 package dry yeast
¾ cup warm water
½ cup mashed potato flakes
3 tablespoons brown sugar,
    firmly packed
1 teaspoon salt
½ teaspoon caraway seed
2 tablespoons cooking oil
1 cup sauerkraut,
    drained and chopped
3 to 3½ cups flour

1. In a large mixing bowl, sprinkle yeast over warm water; stir until dissolved.
2. Blend in potato flakes, brown sugar, salt, caraway seed, oil and sauerkraut.
3. Gradually add flour to make a stiff dough.
4. Knead on floured surface until smooth, approximately 4 minutes.
5. Place in greased bowl. Turn dough to coat all sides. Cover and let rise 1 hour in a warm place until doubled in size.
6. Punch down dough. Place in greased 9x5-inch loaf pan. Cover. Let rise in warm place 1 hour until doubled in size.
7. Preheat oven to 350°.
8. Bake for 55 to 60 minutes until golden brown.
9. Cool in pan, on wire rack, 5 minutes.
10. Remove bread from pan and continue to cool on wire rack.

Dana's Giant Slalom Cookies

Makes 3 dozen

½ cup (1 stick) butter
1 cup chunky peanut butter
¾ cup sugar
¾ cup brown sugar
2 eggs
½ teaspoon vanilla
1¼ teaspoons baking soda
3 cups oats
½ cup chocolate chips

1. Preheat oven to 350°.
2. In a large bowl, cream together butter, peanut butter and sugars.
3. Beat in eggs, vanilla and baking soda.
4. Stir in oats and chocolate chips. Mix thoroughly.
5. Spoon batter (2 tablespoons for each cookie) onto greased cookie sheet and bake 10 to 12 minutes.
6. When done, remove from oven and let cookies sit on cookie sheet 1 minute before removing to wire rack to cool.

Caramel Oat Bars

¾ cup (1½ sticks) butter, softened
1 cup flour
1 cup regular oats
¾ cup brown sugar
½ teaspoon baking soda
¼ teaspoon salt
1 cup semi-sweet chocolate chips
½ cup walnuts, chopped
¾ cup caramel ice cream topping
3 tablespoons flour

Makes 36 1½-inch squares

1. Preheat oven to 350°.
2. In a large bowl, combine butter, flour, oats, brown sugar, baking soda and salt. Mix until crumbly.
3. Press half of mixture into greased 9-inch square pan.
4. Bake for 10 minutes.
5. Remove from oven and sprinkle chocolate chips and walnuts on top of baked portion.
6. Mix caramel topping with 3 tablespoons flour and drizzle over chocolate and walnuts.
7. Sprinkle remaining crumb mixture on top.
8. Bake an additional 20 minutes until golden brown.
9. Remove and cool in pan on wire rack.

Chill to ease cutting.

Coffee Toffee Bars

Cake:

1 cup (2 sticks) butter, softened
1 cup brown sugar, firmly packed
1 teaspoon almond extract
1½ tablespoons instant coffee granules
2¼ cups flour
½ teaspoon baking powder
¼ teaspoon salt
1 cup chocolate chips
½ cup walnuts

Makes 3 dozen

1. Preheat oven to 350°.
2. Cream butter with brown sugar, almond extract and coffee.
3. Gradually add dry ingredients mixing thoroughly after each addition.
4. Stir in chocolate chips and nuts.
5. Press dough into jellyroll pan.
6. Bake for 15 to 18 minutes.
7. Cool in pan on wire rack.
8. Top with Glaze before serving.

Glaze:

1 tablespoon butter, softened
¾ cup confectioner's sugar
1 teaspoon almond extract
½ teaspoon milk

Glaze preparation:

1. Beat together butter, sugar, almond extract and milk.
2. Spread thinly over cooled cake.

Best Ever Carrot Cake

Always a front-runner.

Makes 9 3-inch squares

1½ cups flour
1¼ cups sugar
1½ teaspoons baking soda
1½ teaspoons cinnamon
½ teaspoon salt
2 eggs
⅔ cup oil
1 teaspoon vanilla
¾ cup carrots, grated
⅔ cup coconut
8 ounces crushed pineapple, drained
½ cup walnuts, chopped

1. Preheat oven to 350°.
2. Grease a 9-inch square pan.
3. Mix together flour, sugar, baking soda, cinnamon and salt. Set aside.
4. In another bowl beat together eggs, oil and vanilla.
5. Add carrots, coconut and pineapple. Mix well.
6. Add dry ingredients to carrot mixture. Mix thoroughly.
7. Stir in chopped nuts.
8. Pour into prepared pan and bake for 40 to 45 minutes.
9. Remove to wire rack to cool.
10. Frost with Cream Cheese Frosting.

Cream Cheese Frosting:

3 ounces cream cheese
¼ cup (½ stick) butter
2 cups confectioner's sugar
½ teaspoon vanilla

Cream Cheese Frosting preparation:

1. In a small bowl, cream together cream cheese and butter.
2. Beat in confectioner's sugar.
3. Add vanilla and mix well.

Warm Up Fruit

Enjoy the wonderful aroma while fruits simmer.

Serves 8

2 cups (1-pound can) peach halves
2 cups (1-pound can) pear halves
2 cups (1-pound can) pineapple spears
½ cup orange or ginger marmalade
2 tablespoons butter
1 cinnamon stick
⅛ teaspoon nutmeg
⅛ teaspoon ground cloves

1. Drain fruits, reserving 1½ cups syrup.
2. In a large saucepan, combine marmalade, butter, spices and reserved syrup.
3. Bring to boil; cook 2 to 3 minutes.
4. Reduce heat and gently stir in fruit.
5. Heat 20 minutes.

Serve with ice cream as a dessert or for breakfast with waffles or pancakes.

Macadamia Nut Brownies

A bit more expensive, but worth it.

6 ounces bittersweet chocolate
6 tablespoons unsalted butter
½ cup sugar
¼ cup brown sugar
2 teaspoons vanilla
¾ cup flour
2 tablespoons unsweetened cocoa
½ teaspoon baking powder
¼ teaspoon salt
2 large eggs
¾ cup macadamia nuts, chopped

Makes 16 2-inch squares

1. Preheat oven to 350°.
2. Line the bottom of an 8-inch square pan with foil, then butter the foil.
3. Melt the chocolate, butter and sugars in a saucepan.
4. Remove from heat, stirring until smooth.
5. Let cool slightly, then add vanilla.
6. In a medium size bowl, combine the flour, cocoa, baking powder and salt. Set aside.
7. Beat eggs in a large bowl.
8. Pour cooled chocolate mixture into eggs, stirring to combine.
9. Stir in the flour mixture and nuts. Blend well.
10. Pour entire mixture into prepared pan.
11. Bake 25 to 30 minutes until a wooden pick inserted in the center comes out clean.
12. Cool in pan on a wire rack.

Mint Mousse

2 3-ounce packages lime jello
1½ cups boiling water
1 cup cold water
½ cup Crème de Menthe
1 cup heavy cream

Serves 8 to 10

1. In a large bowl add boiling water to gelatin.
2. Stir until dissolved.
3. Add cold water and Crème de Menthe.
4. Chill until slightly thick.
5. In a separate bowl whip cream until stiff.
6. Fold whipped cream into gelatin.
7. Pour into 10x4½x3-inch loaf pan and refrigerate until set.
8. To remove from pan, immerse bottom and sides of pan in hot water for 5 seconds.

Decorate with rosettes of whipped cream and chocolate shavings.

Fireside Feasting

SAMPLE MENU

Hearthwarming Mulled Wine

Sizzling Steak

Firelight Fritters

Red Ember Salad Mold

Toasted Mashmallows

The welcoming warmth of a snapping fire brightens the dreariest day or darkest night. Indoors or out, firesides create the perfect setting; they invite congenial companions to gather round and share the glowing hospitality. To complete the cozy portrait we must color in great food. These wonderful recipes will greatly contribute to the conviviality. So, throw another log on the fire and let the feasting begin.

Foil Dinner

Serves any number

Every Girl Scout has fond fireside memories.

Dinner per person:
Chicken breast or lean hamburger patty
1 potato, sliced
1 carrot, thinly sliced
a few onion slices
salt and pepper to taste
1 12-inch square aluminum foil

Veggie Dips:
prepared ranch-style dressing
carrot, cucumber, celery and
    green pepper; sliced
broccoli, cauliflower;
    broken into pieces

Strawberry Angel Cake:
1 angel food cake
1 10- to 12-ounce bag
    frozen strawberries
1 12-ounce container
    frozen whipped topping

Dinner preparation:
1. Preheat oven to 350°.
2. Layer meat, potato, carrot and onion on foil.
3. Season with salt and pepper to taste.
4. Fold foil securely into packet.
5. Make 1 packet per person being served.
6. Place packets on cookie sheet.
7. Bake for 40 minutes.
8. Place in preheated crockpot to carry to picnic site. OR bring foil wrapped dinner to picnic site and cook over coals or open fire for 30 minutes.

Dip preparation:
1. Pour ¼ cup dressing in bottom of plastic cup.
2. Add vegetables.
3. Cover cup with plastic wrap and secure with elastic band.
4. Prepare 1 cup per serving.
5. Place in muffin pan for ease in transporting.

Cake preparation:
1. Thaw strawberries and whipped topping at room temperature for 1 hour.
2. Slice and mix strawberries into whipped topping.
3. Frost cake with mixture.

Norsk Kjøttboller (Norwegian Meat Balls)   Makes 30 to 50

Meatballs:

1 pound round steak
½ pound pork
½ pound veal
½ cup bread crumbs
½ cup milk
1 egg
1 teaspoon salt
¼ teaspoon ginger
¼ teaspoon nutmeg
1 large onion, chopped
2 stalks celery, chopped,
  including leaves

Sauce:

2 cans beef consommé
1 can cream of mushroom soup,
  undiluted
3 tablespoons flour

Meatball preparation:

1. Preheat oven to 350°.
2. Meat should be ground several times,
   so it will be fine.
3. Combine meats, bread crumbs and milk.
   Mix thoroughly.
4. Add egg, salt, ginger and nutmeg and
   again mix thoroughly.
5. Put 2 quarts of water, onion and celery
   into a stockpot. Bring water to a boil.
6. Shape meat mixture into 1-inch meatballs.
   Drop meatballs into stockpot. Lower heat
   and simmer 10 minutes.
7. Remove meatballs and place in greased
   baking dish.
8. Make Sauce (below) and pour over
   meatballs. Bake covered for 1 hour.
9. Uncover and bake an additional
   30 minutes until browned.

Sauce preparation:

1. Combine consommé, mushroom soup and
   flour to create a smooth sauce before
   adding to meatballs.

**Meatballs can be made ahead and frozen
before baking.**

Corned Beef Rollups   Makes 18 pieces

2 bunches scallions (approximately 18)
2 4-ounce packages corned beef
1 3-ounce package cream cheese

1. Wash scallions and cut down to 6-inch
   lengths. Discard tops. Dry thoroughly.
2. Separate sliced corned beef into 18 pieces.
3. Spread cream cheese on top of each slice
   of corned beef.
4. Place white end of scallion on edge
   of corned beef slice and roll up.
5. Chill several hours before serving.

Tipsy Brie

Serves 4 to 6

Fast, easy and sure to make sparks fly!

¾ cup pecans, chopped
¼ cup Kahlúa
3 tablespoons brown sugar
14 ounce wheel of Brie

1. In a small bowl microwave pecans 2 to 3 minutes, stirring half-way through, until toasted. Watch carefully or they will burn.
2. Add Kahlúa and brown sugar. Mix together.
3. Remove top rind from Brie and place in serving dish.
4. Top Brie with pecan, Kahlúa and sugar mixture.
5. Microwave until Brie is soft, up to 2 minutes. Monitor this process carefully as Brie softens quickly.

Serve with your favorite cracker.

Red Ember Salad Mold

Serves 10 to 12

1 pound fresh cranberries
1 cup sugar
1 cup water
1 8-ounce package cream cheese, softened
1½ cups cottage cheese
½ teaspoon salt
½ cup prepared horseradish
2 envelopes unflavored gelatin, softened in ½ cup cold water

1. Wash and pick over cranberries.
2. Boil sugar and water together (about 5 minutes).
3. Add cranberries and cook gently, keeping as many cranberries whole as possible. (Set aside a few to outline the mold.)
4. Combine cranberry mixture with cream cheese, cottage cheese, salt and horseradish.
5. Stir in softened gelatin.
6. Pour cranberry mixture into greased 2-quart mold. Chill several hours.

To serve, unmold on serving dish. Garnish with whole cranberries.

Pasta Fagiole Soup

Serves 10 to 12

2 ounces salt pork, ground
¼ cup olive oil
3 cloves garlic, crushed
1 stalk celery, coarsely chopped
2 medium onions, coarsely chopped
1 cup green cabbage, diced
1 quart water
2 quarts chicken stock
1 28-ounce can crushed tomatoes
½ teaspoon salt
½ teaspoon pepper
3 1-pound cans kidney beans, drained
¼ cup parsley, chopped
2 cups pasta, uncooked
1 small head escarole, chopped
grated Romano cheese to taste

1. Place oil and salt pork in heated pot. When salt pork has melted, add garlic, celery, onions and cabbage. Simmer until tender (10 minutes).
2. Add water, chicken stock, tomatoes, salt and pepper. Cook at slow boil for 15 minutes.
3. Add beans and parsley. Cook another 15 minutes.
4. Add 2 cups pasta. Cook until tender. Add escarole.

Serve hot with grated Romano cheese.

Stilton Soup

Serves 4 to 6

1 onion, chopped finely
2 stalks celery, chopped
2½ cups cauliflower, broken into florets
3 tablespoons butter
2 cups chicken broth
1 cup milk
½ teaspoon salt
¼ teaspoon pepper
1 tablespoon cornstarch
2 tablespoons milk
½ cup light cream
¼ pound Stilton cheese, broken into pieces

1. In a medium saucepan cook onion, celery and cauliflower in butter for 10 minutes.
2. Add chicken broth and milk. Cook over low heat 25 minutes until vegetables are soft. Allow to cool slightly.
3. Purée in blender. Add salt and pepper.
4. In a separate saucepan, dissolve cornstarch in 2 tablespoons milk. Bring to a boil to thicken.
5. Add cream and cheese. Stir for 1 minute.
6. Add cheese mixture to puréed mixture and stir together.

Serve hot.

Greek Shrimp

Serves 4

Imagine dining and sipping Retsina in an Athens' taverna.

2 medium onions, chopped
1 clove garlic, crushed
1 tablespoon corn oil
1 16-ounce can stewed tomatoes,
  drained, reserving juice
½ teaspoon basil
1 teaspoon oregano
2 bay leaves
1 teaspoon salt
1 pound medium shrimp
½ cup red wine
4 ounces Feta cheese, crumbled
cooked rice

1. In a large saucepan sauté onion and garlic in oil.
2. Stir in tomatoes, basil, oregano, bay leaves and salt.
3. Add shrimp, reserved tomato juice and wine.
4. Cook until shrimp is cooked, about 3 to 5 minutes.
5. Remove bay leaves and stir in Feta cheese. Serve over rice.

Sizzling Steak

Serves 4 to 6

1½ pounds London broil
1 tablespoon garlic powder
1 tablespoon ginger
½ cup light soy sauce

1. Sprinkle meat with garlic powder and ginger. Place in plastic bag and pour in soy sauce.
2. Seal bag and place in refrigerator for up to 3 days, turning frequently.
3. Cook on grill to desired doneness.

Serve hot or cold.

Loker Herb Chicken

Serves 2 to 4

2 pounds boneless chicken (breasts or legs)
2 lemons
½ teaspoon pepper
1 teaspoon salt
2 teaspoons poultry seasoning
2 teaspoons rosemary
2 teaspoons basil

1. Preheat oven to 350°.
2. Place chicken on greased baking dish.
3. Squeeze 1 lemon over chicken.
4. Mix together pepper, salt, poultry seasoning, rosemary and basil and sprinkle half the mixture over chicken. Bake covered for 30 minutes.
5. Turn chicken over and sprinkle opposite side with remaining lemon and seasonings. Bake uncovered for 20 minutes or until browned.

Microwave Stuffed Chicken Breasts   Serves 6 to 8

1 cup mushrooms, chopped
½ cup onions, chopped
2 tablespoons butter
1 teaspoon instant chicken bouillon
1 cup hot water
3 cups seasoned stuffing mix
4 large boneless chicken breasts
1 cup sour cream
1 10¾-ounce can cream of
    mushroom soup, undiluted

You may use any cream-style soup.

1. Microwave mushrooms, onions and butter
   in a microwavable container on High for
   2 to 3 minutes.
2. Add chicken bouillon, hot water
   and stuffing mix. Mix thoroughly.
3. Pound chicken breasts flat.
4. Place a small scoop of stuffing in the
   center of each breast. Roll breasts
   around stuffing.
5. Place chicken, seam side down,
   in greased 1½-quart baking dish.
6. Place any remaining stuffing on sides
   of dish.
7. Combine sour cream and mushroom
   soup. Pour mixture over chicken breasts.
8. Cover with plastic wrap.
9. Cook on High in microwave for
   10 to 15 minutes.

Tuna Steaks With Ginger Sauce   Serves 2 to 4

1 pound tuna steaks or other firm fish
salt and pepper to taste

Ginger Sauce Marinade:
¼ cup soy sauce
¼ cup teriyaki sauce
2 tablespoons lemon juice
1 clove garlic, crushed
1 tablespoon ginger, grated
lemon slices
parsley

Delicious when grilled over an open flame.

1. Salt and pepper fish steaks.
2. Combine soy sauce, teriyaki sauce, lemon
   juice, garlic and ginger in a bowl. Brush
   both sides of fish with mixture.
3. In a small saucepan boil down remainder
   of marinade until a thick sauce. Set aside.
4. Grill on well greased grill or on a mesh
   grate on top of grill so fish does not fall
   in (or bake in 350° oven).
5. Grill on medium flame for 8 minutes,
   then turn and grill for 5 minutes more
   or until fish flakes.
6. Place cooked fish on serving platter.
7. Pour Ginger Sauce Marinade over fish.

Serve with lemon slices and parsley.

Ralph's Favorite Beans

Serves 6 to 8

An original recipe. They can be your favorite too.

1 pound dried lima beans or
    dried yellow eye beans
1 stalk celery, diced
½ cup molasses
1 14-ounce jar spaghetti sauce
2 cloves garlic, crushed
1 large onion, chopped
1 teaspoon Dijon mustard
⅓ cup brown sugar
1 carrot, chopped
1 16-ounce can stewed tomatoes
1 teaspoon salt
½ teaspoon pepper
water to cover beans

1. Soak beans overnight or boil and let
   stand 1 hour.
2. Preheat oven to 325°.
3. Drain beans and place in large
   casserole dish.
4. Add celery, molasses, spaghetti sauce,
   garlic, onion, mustard, brown sugar,
   carrot, tomatoes, salt and pepper.
5. Add water to cover beans.
6. Cover and bake 4½ to 5 hours.

Serve hot or cold.

Firelight Fritters

Makes 20 2-inch fritters

3 tablespoons oil
1 small onion, finely chopped
¼ cup red pepper, finely chopped
1 cup whole wheat flour
1½ teaspoons rosemary
1 teaspoon baking powder
½ teaspoon pepper
¾ cup water
1 large egg, lightly beaten
1¾ cup whole-kernel corn

1. In a large frypan heat 1 teaspoon oil
   and sauté onion until golden. Stir
   in red pepper and cook until just tender.
   Set aside.
2. In a large bowl, stir together flour,
   rosemary, baking powder and pepper.
3. Add water, egg, corn, sautéd onion and
   red pepper. Stir until well blended.
4. Heat remaining oil in frypan.
5. Drop batter in oil by heaping tablespoonfuls to make 2-inch rounds and fry
   fritters until golden, about 2 minutes per
   side. Serve hot.

**If desired, cool fritters to room temperature, cover
and refrigerate. Then reheat in 400° oven for
10 minutes just before serving.**

Pineapple Upside-Down Cake

A memorable old standby.

Makes 9 2½-inch squares

Topping:
¼ cup (½ stick) butter
½ cup brown sugar
8 canned pineapple spears, drained well
8 canned apricot halves, drained well
9 maraschino cherry halves
8 pecan halves

Topping preparation:
1. Melt butter in a small frypan over low heat.
2. Add brown sugar and stir until well-blended and bubbly.
3. Pour into an 8-inch square cake pan, spreading to cover the bottom.
4. Arrange pineapple spears, apricot halves, cherry halves, and pecan halves on top of sugar mixture in a "sunburst" pattern.
5. Chill in refrigerator while preparing batter.

Batter:
1¼ cups flour
1½ teaspoons baking powder
¼ teaspoon salt
⅓ cup butter
⅔ cup sugar
1 egg
1 teaspoon vanilla
½ cup orange juice

Batter preparation:
1. Preheat oven to 325°.
2. Combine flour, baking powder and salt in a bowl. Set aside.
3. In a large bowl cream together butter and sugar until light and fluffy.
4. Add egg and vanilla and beat until smooth.
5. At low speed, beat in flour mixture alternately with orange juice, beginning and ending with flour; beat only until smooth.
6. Spread batter over fruits in pan.
7. Bake for 40 minutes.
8. Remove from oven. Let stand five minutes.
9. Invert on plate. Serve warm.

Glad-To-Be-Home-Again Chocolate Pudding   Serves 4 to 6

Very welcoming to the palate.

2 squares chocolate
5 tablespoons flour
1½ cups sugar
½ teaspoon salt
3 cups milk
2 eggs, beaten
4 tablespoons butter
2 teaspoons vanilla
whipped cream and shaved chocolate
   for garnish

1. In glass custard cup, melt chocolate in microwave.
2. In saucepan mix flour, sugar, salt and melted chocolate. Slowly add milk. Bring to a boil over medium heat, stirring constantly. Remove from heat.
3. Add small amount of the hot chocolate mixture to beaten eggs and then immediately add the eggs to the chocolate mixture.
4. Reheat, stirring constantly until it thickens. (10 to 15 minutes).
5. Add butter and vanilla. Beat well.
6. Chill several hours before serving.

Serve in fancy glass cups. Top with whipped cream and shaved chocolate.

Apple-Raisin Crunch Pie   Serves 8 to 10

For ultimate enjoyment serve warm in front of a fire.

6 tart apples
¾ cup golden raisins
1 cup water
1 tablespoon flour
1 teaspoon cinnamon
½ teaspoon nutmeg
¼ teaspoon salt
1 cup sugar, divided
½ cup (1 stick) butter, melted
1¼ cups quick oats
½ cup flour
1 unbaked 9-inch pieshell

1. Preheat oven to 450°.
2. Peel, core and slice apples. Place in large saucepan.
3. Add raisins and water. Cook 10 minutes.
4. Mix 1 tablespoon flour, cinnamon, nutmeg, salt and 2 tablespoons of the sugar.
5. Add to the apples, stirring until almost smooth. Bring to a boil.
6. Turn apple filling into pie shell.
7. Combine remaining sugar with butter, oats and the ½ cup flour. Sprinkle over apples.
8. Bake for 10 minutes. Reduce heat to 350° and bake 40 to 45 minutes or until oatmeal topping is golden brown.

Irish Shortbread

Makes 2 dozen

½ cup (1 stick) butter, softened
½ cup brown sugar
1 cup flour

1. Preheat oven to 350°.
2. In a medium bowl mix butter, brown sugar and flour with hands.
3. On a floured board pound dough flat with hands.
4. Roll to ¼-inch thickness.
5. Cut into 2 inch squares.
6. Prick each square with a fork.
7. Bake for 15 minutes on an ungreased cookie sheet.
8. Cool shortbread on wire rack.

Polynesian Barbecue Sauce

½ cup pineapple juice
1 cup soy sauce
½ cup white vinegar
½ cup brown sugar
1 teaspoon garlic powder

1. Combine all ingredients in saucepan and simmer until slightly thickened.

Hearthwarming Mulled Wine

Makes 6 8-ounce servings

The spicy aroma brings to mind a sense of home no matter where you are.

1 cup water
¾ cup sugar
4 cinnamon sticks
4 cloves
5 cardamom seeds
2 lemons, very thinly sliced
3 cups claret or rosé wine
1 cup brandy
1 cup port or Burgundy wine
½ cup blanched almonds
½ cup raisins

1. Boil water, sugar, cinnamon sticks, cloves and cardamom seeds for 5 minutes.
2. Add lemon slices. Cover, and let stand 10 minutes.
3. Strain. Add strained liquid to wines in a large pot.
4. Stir in almonds and raisins.
5. Heat, but DO NOT BOIL. Serve hot.

TREE CUTTING
&
DECORATING

SAMPLE MENU

Christmas Clam Spread

Grandma Gee's Holly Jolly Lulu Paste

Tannenbaum Tomato Zip

Dickens' Cornish Pasties

Santa's Hot Cranapple Cider

Mrs. Claus' Shortbread Cookies

Jingle Bell Fudge

"How dear to me the memory of cutting down the Christmas Tree" and all the goodies that we ate when we began to decorate. There is no better way to enrich this wonderful holiday adventure than to intermingle the aroma of pine with the fragrance of the steaming beverages and savory selections we have listed in this section. They are sure to be heartwarming for tree trimmers of all ages. So, carefully examine all of our holiday favorites and decide which will become part of your treasured tradition.

Grandma Gee's Holly Jolly Lulu Paste   Makes 1½ cups

2 3-ounce packages cream cheese, softened
1 green pepper, finely chopped
1 medium onion, finely chopped
2 eggs, slightly beaten
2 tablespoons sugar
2 tablespoons vinegar
⅛ teaspoon salt

Must be made ahead.

1. In a medium bowl mix cream cheese with green pepper and onion.
2. In a small saucepan cook eggs with sugar and vinegar over medium heat, stirring constantly, until thickened. Add salt.
3. Combine with cream cheese mixture.
4. Refrigerate overnight.

Serve with crackers or chips.

Mexican Spinach Dip   Serves 12

Perfect Christmas colors!

2 tablespoons olive oil
1 medium onion, chopped
2½ tomatoes, chopped
   (reserve half for topping)
1 4-ounce can jalapeño peppers,
   chopped
2 packages frozen chopped spinach,
   thawed and drained
1 small can black olives, drained and sliced
2 cups Monterey Jack cheese, shredded
1 8-ounce package cream cheese,
   cut into small pieces
2 to 3 tablespoons Tabasco sauce
Tortilla chips

1. Preheat oven to 350°.
2. Heat oil in skillet.
3. Add onion and sauté until transparent.
4. Add half the tomatoes, peppers, spinach and three-quarters of the chopped olives.
5. Mix together. Remove from heat.
6. Add Monterey Jack, cream cheese and Tabasco sauce.
7. Spoon into ovenproof serving dish.
8. Bake for 30 minutes until bubbly.
9. Decorate with remaining tomatoes and olives.

Serve with Tortilla chips.

Christmas Clam Spread   Makes 1 cup

Serve in red or green bowl surrounded by holly branches.

1 3-ounce package cream cheese, softened
1 6½-ounce can minced clams, drained
2 scallions, diced
1 tablespoon honey mustard

Must be made ahead.

1. Combine all ingredients, mixing well.
2. Spoon into small serving bowl. Cover and chill several hours before serving.

Serve with assorted crackers.

Christmas Ribbon Jello Salad

A very decorative dish, with 2 to 3 days for preparation.

2 4-ounce packages lime jello
2 4-ounce packages strawberry jello
3 envelopes unflavored gelatin
4 cups boiling water
2½ cups cold water
2 cups milk
1 cup sugar
2 cups sour cream
green food coloring (optional)
1 teaspoon vanilla

**Substitute grape jello and peach jello
and serve for Thanksgiving.**

1. Grease 10x13-inch glass dish.
2. In four individual bowls, dissolve
   1 package of flavored jello at a time in
   1 cup of boiling water plus ½ cup cold
   water. (You may add green food coloring
   to lime jello to intensify color.)
3. In a saucepan, bring 2 cups milk to rolling
   boil. Add sugar and remove from heat.
4. In another bowl, dissolve unflavored
   gelatin in ½ cup cold water. Mix into
   boiled mixture. Add sour cream and whip
   with whisk until smooth.
5. Add the vanilla. Let sit in pan until cool.

Seven layer procedure:

**Each layer must be totally set so it doesn't melt
into next layer.**

1. Layer 1 — one bowl green jello.
2. Layer 2 — 1½ cups white mixture.
3. Layer 3 — one bowl red jello.
4. Layer 4 — 1½ cups white mixture.
5. Layer 5 — second bowl green jello.
6. Layer 6 — 1½ cups white mixture.
7. Layer 7 — second bowl red jello.

REFRIGERATE AND SET UNTIL FIRM
AFTER EACH LAYER.

Curried Rice Salad

Serves 6 to 8

Serve any season — winter or summer.

1 pound rice, cooked
2 scallions, chopped
½ green pepper, chopped
¼ cup green olives, chopped
2 ounces marinated artichoke hearts, chopped
¼ teaspoon curry powder
⅓ cup mayonnaise
1 cup ham chunks
1 cup cantaloupe balls
1 cup honeydew melon balls

Requires some advance preparation.

1. In a large bowl add scallions, pepper, olives and artichokes to cooked rice. Toss.
2. Mix curry powder with mayonnaise. Pour over rice mixture and blend.
3. Refrigerate at least 2 hours.
4. Just before serving stir in ham and fruit.

Fish Soup À La Swede

Serves 6

Discovered by Americans living in Sweden.

1½ pounds frozen cod, thawed and cubed
3 tablespoons butter
1 to 2 leeks, thinly sliced
½ cup celery, chopped and thinly sliced
5 potatoes, peeled and sliced ½-inch thick
5 cups fish stock
½ cup tomato juice
1¼ cups dry white wine
1 cucumber, peeled and sliced ½-inch thick
1 teaspoons salt
1 pound frozen shrimp, thawed

Soup preparation:

1. Melt butter in stock pot.
2. Sauté the leeks, celery and potatoes. DO NOT BROWN.
3. Pour in the fish stock, juice and wine.
4. Simmer for 15 minutes.
5. Add the cod, cucumber and salt.
6. Continue simmering for 8 to 10 minutes.
7. Add shrimp and simmer 5 minutes.
8. Serve soup with spoonful of sauce in middle of bowl.

Sauce:

1 cup mayonnaise
⅔ cup sour cream
⅔ cup parsley, chopped
4 cloves garlic, crushed
1 teaspoon salt
¼ teaspoon black pepper

Sauce preparation:

1. Stir all ingredients together in serving bowl.

After window shopping and enjoying the holiday decorations on the first Sunday of December, the Swedes return home to savor this wonderful soup along with some Christmas cheer — Glögg.

Tannenbaum Tomato Zip

Serves 4

2 cans tomato soup, undiluted
2 10-ounce cans beef broth
½ cup sherry

1. Heat all ingredients in a saucepan.
   DO NOT BOIL.
2. Pour into a warmed thermos and take
   on the road or serve at home with your
   favorite sandwich or salad.

Dickens' Cornish Pasties

Makes 8

"The meal in a pocket" revered by Dickens' schoolboys.

Pastry:

2 cups flour
1 teaspoon salt
⅔ cup chilled butter
6 tablespoons cold water

1. Mix together flour and salt.
2. Cut in butter with pastry blender.
3. Slowly add water until dough forms a ball.
4. Wrap and refrigerate while making filling.

Filling:

½ pound chuck steak, diced
1 medium potato, diced
1 medium onion, diced
½ yellow turnip, diced
1 teaspoon marjoram
1 teaspoon salt
½ teaspoon pepper
½ cup butter (1 stick)
¼ cup fresh parsley
1 egg white

Filling preperation:

1. Preheat oven to 400°.
2. In a large bowl mix together meat,
   potato, onion, turnip, marjoram, salt
   and pepper. Set aside.
3. Remove dough from refrigerator and roll
   out on floured board to ⅛-inch thickness.
   Cut out eight 6-inch circles.
4. Fill each circle with ¼ cup filling and
   dot each with 1 teaspoon butter and
   ½ tablespoon parsley.
5. Moisten perimeter of circle with water
   before folding over and sealing edges.
   Crimp edges with fork.
6. Brush tops with egg white and prick
   with fork.
7. Place on lightly greased pan and bake
   on top shelf for 20 minutes.
8. Reduce heat to 350°, move pan to lower
   shelf, and bake an additional 20 minutes
   until golden brown.
9. Remove from pan when done and cool
   on rack.

Serve hot or cold.

Scalloped Oysters And Scallops   Serves 8 to 10

Makes a good pot-luck supper dish.

½ cup (1 stick) butter, melted
2 cups bread crumbs
1 quart oysters
¾ teaspoon salt
⅜ teaspoon pepper
¾ cup cream
3 tablespoons oyster liquor
1 pint scallops

1. Preheat oven to 425°.
2. Mix melted butter and bread crumbs together, and sprinkle a thin layer in the bottom of a large greased casserole.
3. Layer remaining ingredients in casserole as follows:

   Layer 1 — half the oysters
   Layer 2 — one third of the salt, pepper, cream, liquor and buttered bread crumbs.
   Layer 3 — all the scallops
   Layer 4 — repeat layer 2
   Layer 5 — remaining oysters
   Layer 6 — repeat layer 2.
4. Bake for 30 minutes.

Serve warm. Will stay warm wrapped in newspapers.

Baked Stuffed Eggs   Serves 4 to 6

Eggs
6 hard-boiled eggs
¼ cup (½ stick) butter, melted
1 teaspoon bottled steak sauce
1 teaspoon Dijon mustard
3 scallions with tops, chopped
3 ounces boiled ham, finely chopped
3 cups White Sauce (see below)
1 cup process cheese spread grated
parsley

1. Preheat oven to 350°.
2. Cut eggs lengthwise. Remove yolks.
3. In a large bowl, grate egg yolks and mix with butter, steak sauce, mustard, scallions and ham.
4. Fill egg halves with ham mixture.
5. Arrange in 8x8-inch buttered baking dish.
6. Pour White Sauce over eggs.
7. Sprinkle with cheese and parsley.
8. Cook 30 minutes until bubbly.

White Sauce: (to make 3 cups)
6 tablespoons butter
6 tablespoons flour
3 cups milk
¾ teaspoon salt
¼ teaspoon pepper

White Sauce preparation: Makes 3 cups

1. Melt butter in saucepan over low heat.
2. Add flour and whisk until smooth.
3. Slowly add milk, continuing to whisk.
4. Cook until thickened.
5. Stir in salt and pepper.

Spinach Fritata

Serves 4 to 6

Breakfast, lunch or dinner — quite versatile!

1 tablespoon oil
1 medium onion, chopped
1 10-ounce box frozen spinach,
  thawed and squeezed dry
5 eggs, lightly beaten
¾ pound Muenster cheese, grated
½ teaspoon salt
¼ teaspoon pepper

1. Preheat oven to 350°.
2. In frypan, heat oil and sauté onion until lightly browned.
3. Remove from heat and place in bowl.
4. Stir in spinach, eggs, cheese, salt and pepper.
5. Pour into buttered 9-inch pie plate.
6. Bake 40 to 45 minutes.

Serve hot or cold.

Stuffed Artichokes

Serves 12

Enjoy these artichokes with crusty bread and a glass of wine.

12 artichokes
4 cups bread crumbs
3 eggs
1 4-ounce stick pepperoni, chopped
1 6-ounce can black olives,
  drained and chopped
½ cup plus 2 tablespoons olive oil.

Artichokes can be served covered with tomato sauce.

1. In a large bowl, mix together bread crumbs, eggs, pepperoni, black olives and ½ cup olive oil. Set aside.
2. Clean artichokes by washing with cold water.
3. Snip sharp spikes from leaves and cut off stems.
4. Spread artichokes open and stuff with mixture.
5. Place in large pot with water half-way up artichoke sides.
6. Add 2 tablespoons of oil.
7. Bring to a boil. Simmer 30 to 35 minutes. (When leaves come off easily, artichokes are done.)

Yam Cranberry Casserole

Serves 8 to 10

12 ounces fresh cranberries
1¼ cups sugar
1 small orange, peeled and sliced
¼ cup orange juice or brandy
   (or half of each)
¾ teaspoon cinnamon
¼ teaspoon nutmeg
⅛ teaspoon mace
1 40-ounce can yams, drained
½ cup pecan halves

1. Preheat oven to 375°.
2. Mix cranberries, sugar, orange slices, orange juice or brandy and spices in a 2-quart casserole.
3. Bake, uncovered, for 30 minutes. Stir halfway through cooking.
4. Stir in yams and pecans and bake another 15 minutes.

Serve hot.

Cliff's Cardamom Braided Bread

Makes 2 wreath-shaped loaves

Great for Christmas gift giving! Just add red bow.

1 package rapid-rise yeast
7 cups flour
1½ teaspoons ground cardamom
1 cup sugar
½ teaspoon salt
¼ cup water
2½ cups milk
¾ cup (1½ sticks) butter
1 egg

1. Combine yeast, flour, cardamom, sugar and salt in a very large bowl.
2. Combine water, milk and butter in saucepan and heat to 125°. Add to the bowl of dry ingredients, mixing thoroughly.
3. Add egg, stirring to form a stiff dough.
4. Turn dough out onto a floured surface and knead until smooth and elastic. Add up to 1 cup of additional flour as needed.
5. Place in a very large greased bowl, turning dough to grease top. Cover and let rise in a warm place until doubled in size (about 2 hours).
6. Punch dough down and separate into 6 equal portions. Roll each piece to form "ropes" about 24-inches long.
7. Place 3 "ropes" on greased baking sheet and braid them, forming a circular "wreath." Repeat with other 3 "ropes."
8. Cover and let rise again in a warm place until doubled (about 45 minutes).

9. Preheat oven to 350°.
10. Bake for 30 to 40 minutes until browned, switching loaf positions halfway through baking.
11. Remove to wire rack to cool.

Hanning Bourbon Balls

Makes 3 to 4 dozen

How can anything so easy be so good?!

Dough:
2½ cups vanilla wafers, crushed
1¼ cups pecans, ground
2 tablespoons cocoa
2 tablespoons corn syrup
½ cup bourbon

Rolling mix:
¼ cup confectioner's sugar
2 tablespoons cocoa

1. Combine crushed wafers, nuts and cocoa.
2. Add syrup and bourbon. Mix well.
3. Form dough into small balls.
4. In separate bowl, mix confectioner's sugar and cocoa.
5. Roll balls in cocoa mixture.
6. Store in container at least 24 hours before serving.

Needs no baking.

Mrs. Claus' Shortbread Cookies Makes 2 to 3 dozen

Cut these cookies into trees, stars, angels, . . .

1 cup flour
½ cup cornstarch
½ cup confectioner's sugar
¾ cup butter (1½ sticks)

1. Preheat oven to 300°.
2. Combine flour, cornstarch and sugar in food processor.
3. Add butter and process until dough forms a ball.
4. Remove and roll out on floured board to ⅜-inch thickness.
5. Cut dough into ornament shapes and place on ungreased cookie sheet.
6. Bake 15 minutes or until lightly browned.
7. Remove cookies to wire rack to cool.

Baked cookies freeze well.

Jingle Bell Fudge

Makes 4 dozen 1½-inch pieces

Creamy, smooth, rich and delicious!

3 4-ounce bars German's
  sweet chocolate bar
1 12-ounce package semi-sweet chocolate
2 squares unsweetened baking chocolate
2 cups marshmallow creme
½ cup butter (1 stick)
1 12-ounce can evaporated milk
4½ cups sugar
2 teaspoons vanilla
1 teaspoon salt
2 cups walnuts, coarsely chopped

1. Place chocolates and marshmallow in bowl.
2. In a large saucepan bring butter, milk and sugar to a rolling boil. Boil 5 minutes, stirring constantly.
3. Remove from heat and add vanilla and salt.
4. Pour hot mixture over chocolates and marshmallow and stir until melted.
5. Add nuts and beat until gloss disappears.
6. Pour into a 13x9-inch greased pan and cool until hardened.
7. Cut into 1½-inch squares.

Plum Pudding With Lallah-Rook Sauce

Serves 8 to 10

A Christmas tradition.

Pudding:

1 ¾ cups flour
¼ teaspoon salt
1½ teaspoons baking powder
½ teaspoon cinnamon
⅓ cup butter
½ cup molasses
⅔ cup milk
¼ cup raisins (optional)
¼ cup nuts, chopped (optional)

Pudding preparation:

1. Grease a 1-pound coffee can and line sides with wax paper, extending paper 2-inches beyond top. Grease paper lightly and set aside.
2. In a small bowl combine flour, salt, baking powder and cinnamon.
3. In a small saucepan, melt butter. Let cool slightly.
4. In a large bowl, mix molasses and milk. Add cooled butter along with flour and spices. Mix thoroughly. Add raisins and nuts if desired.
5. Pour batter into prepared coffee can. Cover can with wax paper or foil.
6. Place metal rack in the bottom of a large stockpot. Place coffee can on top of rack. Fill pot, around can, with hot water, to a level one-third up the sides of the can.
7. Heat water to boiling, over high heat. Reduce heat to low, cover pot, and simmer 3 hours.

8. Remove coffee can from water and let sit 5 minutes.
9. Remove cooked pudding from can by first opening bottom with can opener. Remove pudding from can by pulling on wax paper while pushing pudding from opposite end.
10. Cool on wire rack.
11. When ready to serve, slice individual pieces and place on serving dish. Spoon sauce over each serving.

Sauce:

½ cup sugar
1 heaping tablespoon flour
2 cups milk
¼ cup (½ stick) butter
1 egg, beaten

Lallah-Rook Sauce preparation:

1. Mix sugar and flour in saucepan.
2. Add milk, butter and egg.
3. Cook until thick over medium heat, stirring to avoid burning.

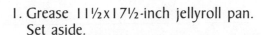

English Toffee

Makes 4 pounds of candy

Once you eat a piece, you won't be able to stop! So, give it as a gift in a fancy tin.

2 cups butter
2 cups sugar
3 cups slivered almonds
6 tablespoons water
12 ounces chocolate chips, melted
1 cup walnuts, chopped

1. Grease 11½x17½-inch jellyroll pan. Set aside.
2. In large saucepan, cook butter, sugar, almonds and water on high heat to boiling.
3. Lower heat to medium high, stirring constantly, continue to boil until mixture becomes a caramel color. (This takes 15 to 20 minutes.)
4. Immediately pour mixture onto greased pan and spread evenly with spoon or spatula. Mixture will harden.
5. Spread melted chocolate on top of caramel.
6. Let chocolate harden slighly. Sprinkle with walnuts and press nuts into chocolate with hands.
7. When cooled and hardened, break into bite size pieces.
8. Store in airtight container.

Aunt Lina's Butter Cookies

Makes 3 to 4 dozen

¾ pound unsalted butter
I cup sugar
2 eggs, separated
3 cups flour, sifted
colored sugar (optional)
chocolate sprinkles (optional)
cinnamon and sugar (optional)
nuts (optional)

1. Preheat oven to 375°.
2. Cream butter. Gradually add sugar and blend until light and fluffy.
3. Add egg yolks one at a time.
4. Gradually cut in flour using a pastry blender.
5. Roll out on board to ¼-inch thickness. Cut with cookie cutters and place on ungreased cookie sheets.
6. Beat egg whites with a fork until foamy. Brush cookies lightly with egg white using pastry brush.
7. Decorate with colored sugar, chocolate sprinkles, cinnamon and sugar or nuts.
8. Bake 10 to 12 minutes or until edges are brown.
9. Cool on wire rack.

Rum Cake

Serves 10 to 12

Cake:

I box deluxe yellow cake mix
¾ cup apricot nectar
¾ cup oil
4 eggs

Cake preparation:

1. Preheat oven to 350°.
2. Grease and flour bundt pan.
3. Mix together cake mix, nectar, oil and eggs. Beat at medium speed for 2 minutes.
4. Pour into prepared bundt pan.
5. Bake for 50 minutes or until cake tester comes out clean.
6. When done, let sit in pan on rack for 5 minutes.
7. Remove from pan and invert on rack.
8. Immediately brush on Rum Sauce. Place wax paper under rack to catch drippings.

Rum Sauce:

½ cup (I stick) butter
I cup sugar
¼ to ½ cup rum

Rum Sauce preparation:

1. Heat until sugar and butter are melted.

Artillery Punch

Makes 20 8-ounce servings

Guaranteed to mow 'em down.

2 litres champagne
½ litre orange brandy
½ litre brandy
1 quart soda water
½ cup lemon juice
2 oranges, sliced

1. Combine all liquids.
2. Pour over ice.
3. Garnish with orange slices.

Wassail Punch

Makes 20 8-ounce servings

This packs a powerful, pleasing punch.

1 orange juice ice ring
1 quart bourbon
1 quart strong tea
1 quart ginger ale
1 12-ounce container frozen orange juice
1 18-ounce container frozen lemonade

1. Put orange juice ring into a punch bowl.
2. Mix remaining ingredients.
3. Pour over ice ring.

Santa's Hot Cranapple Cider

Makes 20 8-ounce servings

Fragrant aromas waft through the house while the cider is simmering.

1 gallon cider
1½ quarts cranberry juice
¼ cup brown sugar
4 3-inch sticks cinnamon
1½ teaspoons whole cloves

1. Combine all ingredients in large pan and heat to boiling.
2. Reduce heat and simmer 20 to 30 minutes.
3. Pour into a warmed thermos and it's ready to go or serve at home from a crock pot.

SUPERBOWL
SPLASH

SAMPLE MENU

Beer and Wine

Touchdown Tapenade

Norman's Minnesota Goalpost Chili

End Zone Muffins

Broccoli Astroturf Salad

Chocolate Chip Cheerleader Cookies

Wide Receiver's Oatmeal Cake

To score points and be a hero at your Superbowl splash, you'll need a few yards of tasty tidbits that can be prepared with maximum efficiency and consumed with minimum fuss. We've come up with recipes to reduce the time you spend huddled over the stove screaming for a time out! These recipes were planned to please even the most irate fans and to ensure that regardless of the final score . . . your party will be a winner.

Touchdown Tapenade

Makes 2 cups

Flavors similar to Salad Niçoise.

1 3½-ounces can tuna
8 ounces small black olives (pitted)
4 anchovies (fillets), rinsed and dried
3 teaspoons capers, rinsed and dried
½ cup olive oil
2 teaspoons lemon juice
1 teaspoon Dijon mustard
½ cup sour cream
⅛ cup fresh parsley, chopped

1. Place tuna, olives, anchovies and capers in a food processor. Blend until thoroughly mixed.
2. Slowly add oil, with motor running.
3. Beat in lemon juice and mustard.
4. Spoon into serving bowl and cool for several hours.
5. Before serving, cover with a thin layer of sour cream sprinkled with fresh parsley.

Serve with toast triangles or crackers.

Baked Cheese With Corn Chips

Serves 6 to 8

2 cups sharp cheddar cheese, grated
1⅓ cups mayonnaise
2 tablespoons onion, grated
1 teaspoon parsley
1 dash Worcestershire sauce
2 egg whites, beaten
1 teaspoon paprika
1 bag corn chips

1. Preheat oven to 350°.
2. In a medium bowl, mix together cheese, mayonnaise, onion, parsley and Worcestershire sauce.
3. In a mixing bowl, beat egg whites until stiff. Fold egg whites into cheese mixture.
4. Sprinkle with paprika.
5. Pour into a greased 8-inch square soufflé dish.
6. Place dish into a larger pan filled with 3 inches of water.
7. Bake 35 minutes or until mixture is firm.
8. Serve with corn chips.

Pepperoncini Cream Cheese Dip   Serves 4 to 6

1 10-ounce jar pepperoncini salad peppers,
   drained and stemmed
1 8-ounce package cream cheese, softened
¼ cup Parmesan cheese, grated
½ cup sour cream

1. In food processor bowl, place
   pepperoncini, cream cheese and
   Parmesan cheese. Pulse until smooth.
2. Blend in sour cream.
3. Place in serving bowl, cover and chill.

Serve dip with toasted pita triangles or garlic chips. Also try this dip as a sandwich spread.

Broccoli Astroturf Salad   Serves 6

Scores big!

1 large bunch fresh broccoli, chopped
   bite-size
1 cup red seedless grapes, halved
1 cup raisins
½ Bermuda onion, sliced
10 strips of bacon, fried and crumbled
1 cup sunflower seeds, toasted.

1. Mix all ingedients in a salad bowl.
2. Serve with Dressing.

Dressing:
1 cup mayonnaise
½ cup sugar
2 tablespoons red wine vinegar

Dressing preparation:
1. Mix all Dressing ingredients and pour
   over salad.

Can be made a day ahead.

Pinto Rice Salad   Serves 8 to 10

2 cups long grain rice
1 quart chicken stock
¼ cup (½ stick) butter
½ cup onion, minced
2 bay leaves
1 28-ounce can pinto, red or black beans
1 bunch scallions, sliced
1 bunch parsley or
   cilantro (coriander), chopped
1 cup pine nuts
1 teaspoon black pepper
1 teaspoon cumin

1. Cook rice in covered saucepan with
   chicken stock, butter, onion and bay
   leaves (26 minutes). Set aside to cool.
2. Drain and rinse beans.
3. In a large serving bowl combine beans
   with scallions, parsley, pine nuts, pepper
   and cumin.
4. Add cooled rice and mix thoroughly.
5. Refrigerate until ready to serve.

Beef Fajita Salad

Serves 4

¡Muy bueno!

1 pound top round steak
⅓ cup lime juice
3 cloves garlic, crushed
½ teaspoon ground cumin
½ teaspoon pepper
6 cups mixed salad greens
2 medium tomatoes, cut into wedges
1 red onion, sliced into rings
1 cup picante sauce
¼ cup low fat plain yogurt

Requires some advance preparation.

1. Trim all fat from steak. Place steak in heavy duty self-locking bag; add lime juice, garlic, cumin and pepper.
2. Marinate 6 to 8 hours.
3. Remove steak from bag and discard marinade.
4. Grill steak over medium coals 2 to 3 minutes on each side or to desired degree of doneness. Cut across grain into thin slices.
5. Arrange equal amounts of salad greens, steak, tomato and onion on serving plates. Serve each salad with ¼ cup picante sauce and 1 tablespoon yogurt.

Superbowl Chicken Chili

Serves 6 to 8

3 whole chicken breasts, split, skinned and diced
1 cup onion, chopped
1 medium green pepper, chopped
2 cloves garlic, crushed
2 tablespoons vegetable oil
1 28-ounce can crushed tomatoes
2 15½-ounce cans pinto beans, drained
1 large jar picante sauce, mild, medium or hot
1 teaspoon chili powder
1 teaspoon cumin
½ teaspoon salt

Optional toppings:
sour cream
cheddar cheese, shredded
scallion, sliced
avocado, diced

1. Cut chicken into ½-inch pieces.
2. In a large stockpot cook chicken, onion, green pepper and garlic in oil until chicken loses its pink color.
3. Add remaining ingredients.
4. Simmer 1 hour.
5. Serve in bowls and add desired toppings.

Can be frozen.

226

Hearty Italian Soup

Serves 6 to 8

Can be stretched to accommodate the whole team.

1 pound bulk Italian sausage
1 medium green pepper, diced
1 medium onion, chopped
2 cloves garlic, crushed
2 28-ounce cans crushed tomatoes
2 quarts water
1 tablespoon granulated chicken bouillon
  OR 3 bouillon cubes
1 tablespoon basil
1 teaspoon oregano
1 cup large macaroni shells, uncooked
Mozzarella cheese, shredded

1. In a large stockpot sauté sausage with green pepper, onion and garlic. Brown and drain.
2. Add tomatoes, water, bouillon, basil, oregano and macaroni shells.
3. Simmer 1 hour.
4. Serve garnished with shredded Mozzarella cheese.

Tofu (Vegetarian) Chili

Serves 8 to 10

Sure to please all your veggie fans.

2 pounds tofu
3 tablespoons peanut butter
1 6-ounce can tomato paste
¼ cup soy sauce
½ cup water
½ teaspoon onion powder
¾ teaspoon garlic powder
2 onions, diced
4 cloves garlic, crushed
1 green pepper, chopped
2 tablespoons oil
1 tablespoon chili powder
1 tablespoon salt
½ teaspoon cumin
5 cups cooked kidney beans
2 cups water

Requires some advance preparation.

1. FREEZE 2 pounds of tofu.
   Freezing tofu changes its consistency, making it chewier as meat would be.
2. Thaw and squeeze out liquid.
3. Tear tofu into bite size pieces and set aside.
4. Mix together peanut butter, tomato paste, soy sauce, water, onion and garlic powders. Cook 1 minute in saucepan until liquid evaporates.
5. In large stockpot cook onion, garlic and green pepper in 2 tablespoons of oil until tender.
6. Add peanut butter mixture, chili powder, salt, cumin, tofu, beans and 2 cups water. Simmer 2 hours. Stir often and add water if needed.

Can be frozen in individual servings.

Red And White Turkey Chili

Serves 6 to 8

A lean team favorite.

2 pounds ground turkey
2 tablespoons vegetable oil
3 cloves garlic, crushed
2 large onions, chopped
2 28-ounce cans stewed tomatoes
1 package taco seasoning mix
1 cup water
1 teaspoon ground cumin
1 teaspoon salt
½ teaspoon pepper
1 teaspoon chili powder
1 16-ounce can red kidney beans, drained
1 16-ounce can white kidney beans, drained
1 8-ounce can black pitted olives (optional)

1. In a large stockpot sauté ground turkey in oil until light brown. Drain.
2. Add garlic and onions. Cook until onions are wilted.
3. Add stewed tomatoes. Stir well.
4. Add taco seasoning, water, cumin, salt, pepper and chili powder. Simmer for 1 hour.
5. Add red and white kidney beans and optional black olives.
6. Simmer for another 30 to 45 minutes, stirring occasionally. (Add more water during cooking if necessary.)

Serve with toasted pita triangles or homemade croutons (sauté bread cubes in olive oil and garlic).

This chili thickens during cooking so check from time to time to see if more liquid should be added.

Superbowl Chili

Serves 6 to 8

Expect a little kick.

1 pound lean ground beef
1 pound lean ground pork
2 15½-ounce cans hot chili beans OR red kidney beans, undrained
1 28-ounce can tomatoes, undrained, diced
2 large onions, chopped
1 green pepper, chopped
3 cloves garlic, crushed
3 tablespoons chili powder
2 tablespoons sugar
1 tablespoon crushed red pepper
3 tablespoons wine vinegar
1 teaspoon ground cumin
2 cups cheddar cheese, shredded
1 cup sour cream

1. In a large stockpot brown beef and pork. Drain fat.
2. Stir in undrained beans, undrained tomatoes, onions, green pepper, garlic, chili powder, sugar, red pepper, wine vinegar and cumin.
3. Cover and simmer for 1 hour stirring frequently to avoid scorching.
4. To serve, ladle the chili into soup bowls. Top each serving with shredded cheese and sour cream.

Norman's Minnesota Goalpost Chili   Serves 12

3 cloves garlic, crushed
2 tablespoons vegetable oil
6 large onions, chopped
3 large green peppers, chopped
4 pounds ground beef
3 pounds canned whole tomatoes, undrained
4 pounds canned kidney beans, drained
2 6-ounce cans tomato paste
¼ cup chili powder
2 teaspoons white vinegar
¼ teaspoon cayenne pepper
3 whole cloves
1 bay leaf
½ teaspoon black pepper

1. In an 8-quart stockpot, sauté garlic in oil until golden.

2. Add onions and green peppers. Sauté until tender.

3. Add ground beef and cook until browned.

4. Add remaining ingredients. Cover and simmer on low heat for at least one hour.

5. Before serving remove bay leaf and serve hot in bowls or mugs.

Chili can be kept on very low heat in a double boiler for hours.

'Kraut And Kielbasa Casserole   Serves 3 to 4

1½ pounds kielbasa
water to cover
1 pound sauerkraut, well drained
½ cup pan broth (from cooked kielbasa)
¼ teaspoon caraway seeds (optional)

1. Preheat oven to 375°.

2. Puncture kielbasa several times with fork (an important step).

3. Barely cover with water and boil in frypan approximately 15 minutes or until thoroughly heated.

4. Remove kielbasa and cut into ¾-inch slices. Set aside.

5. Measure ½ cup pan broth.

6. In a 1½-quart casserole dish, mix sauerkraut, pan broth and caraway seeds.

7. Bake covered for 15 minutes.

8. Remove from oven and mix in kielbasa slices.

9. Cover and return to oven for an additional 15 minutes. Serve hot.

May be reheated the next day. Serve with rye or pumpernickel bread or rolls.

End Zone Muffins

Serve with chili or any zesty entrée.

1 cup flour
¾ cup cornmeal
¼ cup sugar
½ teaspoon baking soda
¼ teaspoon salt
1 cup cheddar cheese, shredded
½ cup butter, melted
1 cup sour cream
1 egg, slightly beaten

Makes 12 muffins

1. Preheat oven to 375°. Grease muffin pan.
2. In large bowl combine dry ingredients with cheese.
3. In separate bowl combine butter, sour cream and egg.
4. Stir flour mixture into butter mixture until moistened.
5. Spoon into prepared muffin pan.
6. Bake 25 to 30 minutes until golden.
7. Remove muffins to rack and cool.

Serve warm.

Cheesy Herb Muffins

1¾ cups whole wheat flour
1 tablespoon baking powder
1 teaspoon basil
½ teaspoon thyme
½ teaspoon oregano
½ teaspoon pepper
½ teaspoon dry mustard
¼ teaspoon salt
1¼ cups skim milk OR water
2 large egg whites, lightly beaten
1 cup cheddar cheese, shredded

Makes 12 muffins

1. Preheat oven to 400°.
2. In a large bowl, combine flour, baking powder, basil, thyme, oregano, pepper, mustard and salt.
3. Add milk and egg whites. Stir just until dry ingredients are moistened.
4. Set aside 2 tablespoons cheese.
5. Fold remaining cheese into batter.
6. Grease the cups and the top of a muffin pan.
7. Fill cups two-thirds full and sprinkle batter with reserved cheese.
8. Bake for 20 minutes or until golden.
9. Remove muffins to wire rack to cool.

Serve warm.

Wide Receiver's Oatmeal Cake

Makes 2 cakes, one 9x13-inch and one 9x9-inch OR one larger cake 11¼x15¾-inch.

3 cups boiling water
1 cup quick cooking oats
1 cup (2 sticks) butter
2 cups light brown sugar, packed
2 cups white sugar
4 eggs
3 cups flour
2 teaspoons nutmeg
2 teaspoons cinnamon
2 teaspoons baking soda
2 teaspoons salt

1. Preheat oven to 350°.
2. Grease and flour only the bottoms of the baking pans.
3. In a small bowl, pour boiling water over oats. Let stand 20 minutes or until cool.
4. In a large bowl, cream together butter, sugars and eggs.
5. Add cooled oatmeal mixture.
6. Sift together flour, nutmeg, cinnamon, baking soda and salt. Add to the creamed mixture. Mix thoroughly.
7. Pour into prepared pan and bake for 40 to 45 minutes or until cake tester inserted into center comes out clean. Remove cake from oven, cool slightly and frost with Coconut Frosting.

Coconut Frosting:
½ cup butter (1 stick)
1 cup light brown sugar
1 cup flaked coconut
½ cup walnuts, chopped
½ teaspoon vanilla
⅛ cup milk

Best made the day before serving. Freezes well.

Frosting preparation:
1. In saucepan combine all Frosting ingredients and bring to a boil. Continue to boil for one minute.
2. Spread thinly over warm cake.
3. Place frosted cake under broiler (6 to 8 inches from the heat) until the frosting bubbles. WATCH CAREFULLY — it takes less than a minute for Frosting to bubble and brown.
4. Cool cake in pan on wire rack.

Pumpkin Ice Cream Pie

Serves 6 to 8

1 cup pumpkin, cooked and mashed
½ cup brown sugar
½ teaspoon salt
½ teaspoon cinnamon
½ teaspoon ginger
¼ teaspoon nutmeg
1 quart vanilla ice cream, softened
1 graham cracker pie crust

1. In a medium bowl, combine pumpkin and spices.
2. Stir in softened ice cream and blend well.
3. Spoon mixture into crust and freeze several hours before serving.

Chocolate Chip Cheerleader Cookies Makes 2 dozen

Time out! These cheerleader cookies are sure to draw a response from the crowd.

½ cup (1 stick) butter
½ cup white sugar
½ cup brown sugar
1 egg
½ teaspoon vanilla
1 cup flour
1¼ cups oats, ground in blender
   until powdery
¼ teaspoon salt
½ teaspoon baking powder
½ teaspoon baking soda
6 ounces chocolate chips
2 ounces milk chocolate, grated
¾ cup nuts, chopped

1. Preheat oven to 375°.
2. Cream butter and sugars.
3. Add egg and vanilla. Blend well.
4. Mix together flour, oats, salt, baking powder and baking soda.
5. Combine wet and dry ingredients, and add chocolate chips, grated chocolate and nuts. Mix well.
6. Shape dough into golf-ball sized rounds and place on ungreased cookie sheet, 2 inches apart.
7. Bake for 10 to 12 minutes. DO NOT OVERBAKE.
8. Cool cookies on wire rack.

Apple Squares

Makes 2 dozen 2-inch squares

3 eggs
1¾ cups sugar
2 cups flour
1 teaspoon baking powder
1 teaspoon cinnamon
1 teaspoon salt
1 teaspoon vanilla
1 cup cooking oil
2 cups apples, (about 3 apples), pared and thinly sliced
confectioner's sugar

1. Preheat oven to 350°.
2. In a large bowl, beat eggs. Gradually add sugar, beating until fluffy.
3. Add flour, baking powder, cinnamon and salt. Mix well.
4. Stir in vanilla and oil.
5. Fold in sliced apples.
6. Pour into a greased 9x13-inch pan.
7. Bake for 35 to 40 minutes.
8. When done, cool in pan on wire rack.
9. Sprinkle with confectioner's sugar before serving.

This cake freezes very well.

INDEX

234

NOTES

NOTES

NOTES

NOTES

NOTES

NOTES

NOTES

NOTES